S0-DON-556

New Directions for
Student Services

John H. Schuh
EDITOR-IN-CHIEF

Elizabeth J. Whitt
ASSOCIATE EDITOR

Gender Identity and Sexual Orientation

Research, Policy, and Personal Perspectives

Ronni L. Sanlo

EDITOR

Number 111 • Fall 2005
Jossey-Bass
San Francisco

GENDER IDENTITY AND SEXUAL ORIENTATION: RESEARCH, POLICY, AND PERSONAL PERSPECTIVES
Ronni L. Sanlo (ed.)
New Directions for Student Services, no. 111
John H. Schuh, Editor-in-Chief
Elizabeth J. Whitt, Associate Editor

NEW DIRECTIONS FOR STUDENT SERVICES (ISSN 0164-7970, e-ISSN 1536-0695) is part of The Jossey-Bass Higher and Adult Education Series and is published quarterly by Wiley Subscription Services, Inc., A Wiley Company, at Jossey-Bass, 989 Market Street, San Francisco, California 94103-1741. Periodicals Postage Paid at San Francisco, California, and at additional mailing offices. POSTMASTER: Send address changes to New Directions for Student Services, Jossey-Bass, 989 Market Street, San Francisco, California 94103-1741.

New Directions for Student Services is indexed in College Student Personnel Abstracts and Contents Pages in Education.

Microfilm copies of issues and articles are available in 16mm and 35mm, as well as microfiche in 105mm, through University Microfilms Inc., 300 North Zeeb Road, Ann Arbor, Michigan 48106-1346.

SUBSCRIPTIONS cost $75 for individuals and $170 for institutions, agencies, and libraries. See ordering information page at end of book.

EDITORIAL CORRESPONDENCE should be sent to the Editor-in-Chief, John H. Schuh, N 243 Lagomarcino Hall, Iowa State University, Ames, Iowa 50011.

www.josseybass.com

CONTENTS

EDITOR'S NOTES

The police raid at the Stonewall Inn in New York City occurred in June 1969. As in many cities, New York's lesbian and gay citizens were often harassed by police as they entered or exited the local gay nightclubs. That night in June, and for five nights thereafter, the patrons of the Stonewall bar decided to fight back, igniting what some suggest was the start of the modern lesbian, gay, bisexual, transgender (LGBT) civil rights movement. Gay Liberation Front organizations quickly emerged on college campuses around the country. By 1971, the demands and the visibility of gay and lesbian activists led to the opening at the University of Michigan of what would become the first LGBT campus resource center. The new unit was called the Human Sexuality Office.

The riots at the Stonewall had been preceded by the sting operations of what was called the Johns Committee in three of Florida's public universities (University of Florida, Florida State University, the University of South Florida). In 1958, the Florida Legislative Investigative Committee, chaired by Senator Charley Johns, was charged with obtaining information about the NAACP and its members; the NAACP was assumed by some Florida legislators to be a Communist organization. The NAACP refused to cooperate with the Johns Committee, so the Committee turned its sights on homosexuals in higher education. Many professors and students were accused, accurately or not, of being homosexuals. Some were forced to leave higher education. Some committed suicide. When the report of the Johns Committee was presented to the Florida Legislature in 1964, it was considered to be the hottest item on the pornographic market that year. The Legislature called the report crude and disgusting, threw it out, and disbanded the Johns Committee, but the damage to the lives and reputations of many faculty and students had already occurred.

In 1965 I became a first-year student at the University of Florida. I had heard about the scare by the Johns Committee and I vowed that no one would find out about me. To avoid being labeled a lesbian, I taunted and harassed the three gay male students I knew at the university. Their lives and mine were a living hell, and no one on campus protected us or assured us that we were valued or that we mattered. I remained closeted, ashamed, and isolated for another fourteen years.

In 1994 I became the director of the University of Michigan's LGBT center. Five or six other such centers existed at that time. Today there are

---

This issue is dedicated to Amanda Hafleigh (1985–2004).

nearly one hundred such centers nationwide, and the position of LGBT center director is an emerging functional area in student affairs.

In addition, from the time Michigan opened its LGBT office in 1971, and especially since the mid-1990s, more than five hundred colleges and universities have added sexual orientation to their nondiscrimination policies; only fifteen states have done the same. It is ironic that many of the institutions that have included sexual orientation in their nondiscrimination policies are located in states without similar protections. In thirty-five states, higher education faculty and staff may be fired from their jobs for no reason other than their sexual orientation or gender identity. As a result, regardless of institutional policies, many faculty and staff are unwilling to be open, avoid disclosing their nonheterosexual orientation to anyone, and are neither willing nor able to be role models for students struggling with their own sexual identity issues. For example, few LGBT senior student affairs officers (SSAOs) are willing to be open; many graduate preparation programs in student affairs are uninformed about how to include LGBT issues, theories, and services into their curricula; and LGBT student affairs professionals are often overlooked for advancement into senior positions in student affairs.

This volume is designed to provide an understanding of the current research and policies as institutions of higher education search for ways both to provide services to lesbian, gay, bisexual, and transgender college students and to nurture faculty and staff. The scholars and practitioners whose chapters appear in this volume hope that LGBT SSAOs may one day feel safe enough to be open about their own identities and serve as effective role models and mentors; that LGBT inclusion in graduate preparation curricula is seamless and ordinary; and that SSAOs realize that LGBT center directors are experienced generalists on campus, serving students of all races, abilities, socioeconomic classes, genders, and ages, and knowledgeable about every area of campus—from residential life and financial aid to health care, academic advising, and more.

Although there are many areas to be addressed in understanding LGBT work on campus, no road maps are available that clearly delineate how higher education and student affairs administrators should proceed. Some general areas are, however, critical to broadening our understanding: longitudinal research about the lives and retention issues of LGBT students; development of appropriate materials for graduate-level curricula for preparing student affairs professionals; services and safe spaces for transgender students, faculty, and staff; and services, programs, and development activities to ensure financial support of LGBT-related activities. Work to study and address LGBT issues is still relatively new to higher education and student affairs. We make history each time a new center opens, a campus conducts a climate survey, or an LGBT-related dissertation is approved or a study is funded. This volume, therefore, is designed to help student affairs professionals understand some of the more critical issues of LGBT students and staff.

The first three chapters of the volume address policy and research. Policies create a foundation of inclusion; they are the reflection that tells people they were expected on that campus, regardless of whether or not they are open about their identity or identities. In Chapter One, Zemsky and Sanlo document policies that include sexual orientation as well as gender identity or gender expression. These policies are only the beginning of the work an institution must do to make a campus safe and welcoming for LGBT students, staff, and faculty. Policies must be in place to offer domestic partner benefits, for example, as well as inclusion in curricula and services. Because sexual orientation is a characteristic that one cannot see in another (although because of societal stereotypes, we *think* we can guess a person's sexual orientation), LGBT people might not come forward to ask for inclusion or to talk about problems in the workplace, the residence hall, or the classroom.

In Chapter Two, Rankin describes her national study of more than one thousand LGBT students, documenting their experiences of harassment and discrimination. The Rankin study, one of the first and largest endeavors of its kind, examines the social climates on many campuses to understand what LGBT students, faculty, and staff see, hear, and experience. Based on the results of the study, Rankin offers suggestions for moving campuses forward toward understanding and including LGBT students, faculty, and staff.

In Chapter Three, Bilodeau and Renn describe their ongoing research regarding sexual orientation and gender identity or gender expression development. Although several models describe sexual identity development, tremendous fluidity, complexities, and contradictions exist among these models. Bilodeau and Renn examine and compare current models and their characteristics, then describe possibilities for new models, not only for sexual orientation but also for bisexual and gender identities.

In Chapter Four, Poynter and Washington describe the complex intersections of race, faith, and sexual orientation. They indicate that an underlying assumption in many populations is that sexual orientation is an issue strictly related to whites. Such an assumption renders LGBT people of color particularly invisible and can exclude them from both communities. The authors identify issues related to these intersecting multiple identities and offer suggestions to student affairs professionals about how to create welcoming environments for people with both visible and invisible identities, such as, for example, a black lesbian.

Issues and experiences of transgender students are hot topics for discussion on college campuses and at meetings of student affairs professional associations. In Chapter Five, Beemyn, Curtis, Davis, and Tubbs define terminology commonly associated with transgender experiences. Beemyn examines services to transgender students on campus. Davis draws from his experiences as a transgender graduate student and founder of the FTM Alliance of Los Angeles, where he creates curricula about gender identity for public schools. Curtis and Tubbs both provide services to transgender students on their campuses, and Tubbs developed policies regarding trans-gender students in the residence halls when most institutions addressed transgender residency on a case-by-case basis.

Community colleges address issues of LGBT students differently, and perhaps with more difficulty, than four-year institutions. In Chapter Six, Ivory describes the needs and experiences of LGBT students, faculty, and staff at a community college where the challenges begin with the transient population of the institution.

Although about one hundred LGBT resource centers exist on college campuses, the trend appears to be the addition of such centers. In Chapter Seven, Ryan describes the development of a university LGBT center. Challenges, issues, processes, programs, and services are described, and the use of the Council for the Advancement of Standards (CAS) for LGBT center development is discussed.

In Chapter Eight, Talbot and Viento describe a model for the inclusion of LGBT issues into student affairs graduate preparation curricula. Inclusion of LGBT students, theories, and issues in student affairs preparation is imperative if new professionals are to serve all college students effectively.

In Chapters Nine and Ten, student affairs professionals share experiences with issues faced by LGBT students, faculty, and staff from their own perspectives. In Chapter Nine, Roper describes his journey to understanding the importance of including LGBT people in his considerations as he moved up the administrative ladder to become the vice provost for student affairs at a public research university. He shares the ways in which he became an ally for LGBT people. Chapter Ten begins with Albin sharing her journey from closeted new professional to midlevel manager and open lesbian. Her story incorporates her experiences with her professional association, how she came to sit on the national board of that association, and what she as a lesbian in student affairs expects from professional associations. Dungy describes her experiences as she came to understand the issues of LGBT people and how she, like Roper, became an ally. She also explains, from her perspective as the executive director of the National Association of Student Personnel Administrators (NASPA), what professional student affairs associations must do to maintain a commitment to include LGBT members.

In 1994, at the age of 47, I was a nontraditional-age new professional in student affairs. The next year, I created a graduation celebration at the University of Michigan to honor the lives and achievements of LGBT students. I called it Lavender Graduation because lavender is the color used—along with the pink triangle and the rainbow flag—to signify the LGBT movement. Since that first Lavender Graduation, I've witnessed hundreds of LGBT students celebrate their commencement at Lavender Graduation ceremonies at many institutions, and LGBT centers are opening their doors at campuses across the country, including my alma mater, the University of Florida.

The authors of the chapters in this volume and I hope this issue, with its rich resources, courageous ideas, and visionary suggestions by forward-thinking professionals, is but one more step on that lavender-brick road to full inclusion of LGBT people in student affairs and higher education.

Ronni L. Sanlo
Editor

RONNI L. SANLO is director of the UCLA LGBT Campus Resource Center, a faculty in residence, and a lecturer in the UCLA Graduate School of Education.

This chapter provides an overview of nondiscrimination policies that include sexual orientation and gender identity and addresses how such policies might be used to improve campus climates for LGBT students, faculty, and staff.

Do Policies Matter?

Beth Zemsky, Ronni L. Sanlo

Lesbian, gay, bisexual, and transgender (LGBT) students, faculty, and staff have always been a vital part of the history of American universities (Wrathall, 1993). Homophobia, transphobia, and heterosexism in the academy have, however, led to discrimination, harassment, and violence, as well as to more subtle incidents of exclusion, marginalization, and silence (Dilley, 2002). Academic environments inhospitable to LGBT students, faculty, and staff also have stilted scholarship, teaching, and outreach in the pursuit of knowledge about LGBT lives (McNaron, 1996).

The 1990s witnessed a rapid increase in attention to LGBT campus climate issues, including the creation of LGBT centers at many institutions. The work of task forces and resource centers contributed to significant changes for LGBT faculty, staff, and students (Beemyn, 2002; Rankin, 1998). These changes include nondiscrimination policies inclusive of sexual orientation and gender identity or gender expression (the terms commonly used to describe transgender experiences), domestic partner benefits, inclusion of LGBT issues in campus diversity initiatives, and increased interest in LGBT studies. In addition, policies and programs to support LGBT students have been integrated throughout student affairs units on many campuses (Zemsky, 2004). Despite these changes, however, many campuses remain challenging environments for LGBT community members.

This chapter provides an overview of nondiscrimination policies that address sexual orientation and gender identity or gender expression and the impact they can have on campus climates for LGBT faculty, staff, and students.

The Context

Discrimination is based on prejudicial, usually negative, beliefs or stereotypes that individuals have about groups of people. Discrimination can be defined as treating a person unfairly according to factors unrelated to ability or potential (Legal Definitions, 2005). In the workplace, discrimination can be manifested in disparate treatment in hiring, delegation of work assignments, compensation, performance evaluation, and promotion opportunities. In many places in the United States, LGBT people are not considered a class to be protected by nondiscrimination statutes and policies, so workplace discrimination based on sexual orientation and gender identity or gender expression may occur with no legal recourse for those who experience it (Brown, 2004). "Protected class" identifies individuals who are members of groups against whom past systemic discrimination has been recognized. Legal recourse is available to these individuals if discrimination is demonstrated. In civil rights law, discrimination is defined as unfavorable or unfair treatment of a person or class of persons in comparison to others who are not members of the protected class (Tobias and Sauter, n.d.). According to federal nondiscrimination laws, discrimination on the basis of race, age, sex, national origin, religion, ability status, and veteran status with respect to any term, condition, or privilege of employment is illegal (U.S. Equal Employment Opportunity Commission, 2005).

However, the federal government and thirty-five states do not include sexual orientation, and forty-five states do not include gender identity or gender expression in these laws (National Gay and Lesbian Task Force, 2005a). Only fifteen states include sexual orientation in nondiscrimination laws (see Exhibit 1.1). Of these, only five states also prohibit discrimination based on gender identity or gender expression (National Gay and Lesbian Task Force, 2004).

According to the National Gay and Lesbian Task Force's Policy Institute, even if all of the approximately 250 local municipalities that include sexual orientation in nondiscrimination policies are included in these totals, fewer than one-half of all Americans live in jurisdictions in which even overt discrimination against LGB people would be prohibited. Only 27 percent of Americans live in locations that also would prohibit discrimination based on gender identity or gender expression (Cahill, 2005). In addition, only one state (Massachusetts) allows same-sex marriage, and three states (Vermont, California, and New Jersey) allow access to relationship recognition and benefits through same-sex civil union statutes.

At the same time, as of November 2004, seventeen states had passed constitutional amendments banning same-sex marriage, and many others had statutes opposing same-sex marriage (NGLTF, 2005b). Thus, the lack of federal, state, and local laws that protect LGBT people from discrimination in employment persists despite widespread support for equal rights in job opportunities. Since the early 1990s, polls have shown widespread public

Exhibit 1.1. States with Sexual Orientation and Gender Identity Nondiscrimination Policies and Years of Inclusion

Sexual Orientation and Gender Identity
Minnesota, 1993
Rhode Island, 2001
New Mexico, 2003
California, 2003
Illinois, 2005

Sexual Orientation Only
Wisconsin, 1982
Massachusetts, 1989
Connecticut, 1991
Hawaii, 1991
New Jersey, 1992
Vermont, 1992
New Hampshire, 1997
Nevada, 1999
Maryland, 2001
New York, 2002

Source: NGLTF, 2005

support for equal employment rights for people regardless of sexual orientation (Henry J. Kaiser Family Foundation, 2001; Yang, 1999).

The lack of legal protection from discrimination in the workplace and the widespread implementation of laws denying equal protection and equal benefits to same-sex couples can have a chilling effect on whether students, faculty, and staff choose to be open about their sexual identities on campus. Even if a campus is located in a state or municipality that has an inclusive anti-discrimination law, the patchwork distribution of these laws means that students, faculty, and staff might not feel safe to be "out." For example, when LGBT students graduate or faculty and staff members seek to leave an institution for an opportunity in another job location that does not have an inclusive nondiscrimination law, previous public disclosures about their sexual identity can affect their future educational or employment opportunities and the direction of their careers.

Many employers, including 415 of Fortune 500 companies, address the lack of national and local nondiscrimination laws by implementing equal opportunity workplace policies to protect their LGBT employees from discrimination (Human Rights Campaign, 2005). Equal opportunity policies attempt to provide equal access and opportunity to all of an organization's employees regardless of identity characteristics. Because opponents to inclusive policies often claim that such policies will force an organization to establish quotas and prescribe hiring LGBT people, we must differentiate between equal opportunity and affirmative action policies. Affirmative action policies create results-oriented plans to increase the diversity of the workforce, particularly in race and sex. Affirmative action strategies were created as a remedy for past discrimination and lack of equal opportunities, and they set numerical goals for percentage of women and people of color in the workforce. These goals are not quotas, and there is no direct penalty for not meeting the goals (Legal Definitions, 2005). Affirmative action policies and plans typically have not included LGBT people.

According to the Human Rights Campaign (2005), in March 2005, 2,878 employers had nondiscrimination policies that included sexual orientation. As the trend to include sexual orientation and gender identity or gender expression in equal opportunity policies has expanded throughout many sectors of the economy, they also have begun to take root in institutions of higher education (Raeburn, 2004).

Development of Campus Equal Opportunity Policies

In the late 1980s, LGBT students, faculty, and staff began to become more visible and more demanding of their rights and academic freedom on college campuses (Dilley, 2002). This increased visibility was assisted by, and indeed often followed, colleges and universities explicitly adding a clause to their equal opportunity statements protecting against workplace and academic discrimination associated with sexual orientation (Raeburn, 2004; Zemsky, 2004). The existence of these inclusive equal opportunity policies encouraged LGBT faculty and staff to disclose their sexual orientation publicly without overt risk to their jobs, their academic advancement, or their professional standing (McNaron, 1996). Indeed, a 2000 survey of campuses with LGBT offices found that 100 percent of these centers were located on campuses with equal opportunity statements inclusive of sexual orientation, and 39 percent were located in states with inclusive human rights laws (Sanlo, 2000).

For those campuses that have equal opportunity policies, there appears to be decreased risk for LGBT faculty and staff who disclose their sexual orientation publicly. This can significantly alter the nature of the work to address LGBT issues on these campus. For about fifteen years after the 1969 Stonewall rebellion in New York, LGBT students carried most of the charge to improve campus climates for LGBT issues (Dilley, 2002). At times, their work to improve their institutions distracted them from their primary function on campus, that is, to be students and to graduate. As a result, LGBT students often suffered the negative consequences of attempts to alter institutional systems that were larger, more complicated, and more entrenched than their resources allowed them to influence. Once campuses began to implement equal opportunity statements inclusive of sexual orientation, LGBT students were no longer the only voices challenging the injustices that were occurring; faculty and staff began to speak out as well. Collaborations began and the potential for long-term change in institutional climates increased (Zemsky, 2004).

In general, though such policies may be used as grounds for formal complaints and lawsuits, they are more often used as symbols of institutional commitment to equality. Discriminatory institutional practices can be challenged successfully by pointing to the existence of a nondiscrimination statement that includes LGBT people and reminding those involved that such practices violate that policy and could be the basis for a successful complaint. Seldom does such a complaint have to materialize for the discriminatory practice to be modified or dropped altogether. In other words, nondiscrimination policies provide both a "stick" and a "carrot" for holding institutions to their commitments to diversity and equality.

Implications for Student Affairs

The effects of changes in equal opportunity policies can be seen in a variety of ways in student affairs divisions. Students and staff alike often expect the policies to be recognized and honored, which can influence programs, services, and the day-to-day work in every functional area (see the Appendix at the end of this chapter for examples of policies). It is often through student affairs that students experience the personal welcome and consideration and celebration of who they are. It is student affairs professionals from whom students get the message that they matter, reminding students that they were expected at our institutions. Examples of student affairs practices in keeping with equal opportunity policies include advocacy for transgender health benefits for employees and students, for providing LGBT-related training within student affairs and throughout the institution, and for changing the phrase *married student housing* to *family housing*.

Examples of institution-wide policies consistent with nondiscrimination statements include advocacy for domestic partner benefits and relatively speedy attention to and resolution of individual complaints of LGBT discrimination (such as unfair hiring and promotion practices, unfair grading practices) that, without an institutional policy allowing the affected individual or individuals to file a complaint, might otherwise languish.

For institutions without inclusive policies, the Council for the Advancement of Standards in Higher Education (CAS) offers excellent examples of services for LGBT students and staff (CAS, 2001). The Council calls for, and describes, the inclusion of sexual orientation and gender identity or gender expression within the context of each functional area in student affairs, including graduate preparation programs.

Conclusion

The inclusion of sexual orientation and gender identity or gender expression in institutional nondiscrimination policies lends LGBT issues importance that encourages discussion about such issues in a variety of workplace and classroom settings. In addition, the extension of protection from discrimination to LGBT people at an institution provides a powerful rationale for conducting climate surveys to determine the extent of discrimination at the institution and for creating entities to monitor and correct possible LGBT-related inequities. Such surveys and groups can usefully supplement the work of a resource center or provide crucial impetus for the creation of a center where none exists. At a minimum, the process of achieving LGBT inclusion in nondiscrimination policies opens, or provides an opening for, unprecedented dialogue about the experiences of LGBT people on a given campus.

Appendix: Examples of Policies of Inclusion

This appendix presents excerpts from the policies of inclusion developed by a variety of types of institutions.

Small Public Institution: Oregon State University

Oregon State University, as an institution of higher education and as a community of scholars, is committed to the elimination of discrimination and the provision of equal opportunity in education and employment.

Oregon State University, in compliance with state and federal laws and regulations, does not discriminate on the basis of race, color, national origin, religion, sex, sexual orientation, marital status, age, disability or veteran's status in any of its policies, procedures, or practices. This nondiscrimination policy covers admission and access to, and treatment and employment in, University programs and activities, including but not limited to academic admissions, financial aid, educational services, and employment.

Oregon State University's policies are designed to ensure that all applicants receive fair consideration for employment and that employees are treated equitably. This includes but is not limited to:

1. Recruiting, hiring, training, and promoting persons in all job titles, without regard to race, color, religion, sex, or national origin, except where sex is a bona fide occupational qualification;
2. Basing decisions on employment so as to further the principle of equal employment opportunity;
3. Insuring that promotion decisions are in accordance with principles of equal employment opportunity by imposing only valid requirements for promotional opportunity; and
4. Insuring that all personnel actions, such as compensation, benefits, transfers, layoffs, returns from layoff, OSU sponsored training, education, tuition assistance and social and recreation programs, will be administered without regard to race, color, national origin, religion, sex, sexual orientation, marital status, age, disability or veteran's status.

It is the intent of the University that all members of the community— employees and students—share the responsibility for making equal employment opportunity and affirmative action dynamic aspects of University life.

[http://oregonstate.edu/dept/affact/policy.html]

Private Institution: Syracuse University

Equal Opportunity Statement

Syracuse University supports equal opportunity regardless of race, color, national origin, or gender, and in compliance with title VI of the Civil Rights Act of 1964 and Title IX of the Education Amendments of 1972, does not discriminate on the basis of race, color, national origin, or gender.

Non-Discrimination Policy:

Syracuse University is an equal-opportunity, affirmative-action institution. We do not discriminate on the basis of race, creed, color, gender, national origin, religion, marital status, age, disability, sexual orientation, or status as a disabled veteran or a veteran of the Vietnam era to any extent discrimination is prohibited by law. This nondiscrimination policy covers admissions, employment, and access to and treatment in University programs, services, and activities. [http://www.syr.edu/policies/nondiscrimination.html]

Large Public Institution That Also Includes Gender Identity: The University of Minnesota

Diversity, Equal Employment Opportunity, and Affirmative Action

Subd. 1. Commitment of Purpose. Consistent with its academic mission and standards, the University of Minnesota is committed to achieving excellence through diversity. As a community of faculty, staff, and students engaged in research, scholarship, artistic activity, teaching and learning, or activities which support them, the University fosters an environment that is diverse, humane, and hospitable. As an institution, the University is a global enterprise which serves the state, the nation, and the world through its outreach and public service, and in partnership with community groups.

Subd. 2. Goals. The University shall seek to:

1. Provide equal access and opportunity to its programs, facilities, and employment without regard to race, color, creed, religion, national origin, sex, age, marital status, disability, public assistance status, veteran status or sexual orientation;
2. Advocate and practice affirmative action, including the use of recruiting and search processes to enhance participation of racial minorities, women, persons with a disability, and Vietnam era veterans;
3. Establish and nurture an environment that actively acknowledges and values diversity and is free from racism, sexism, and other forms of prejudice, intolerance, or harassment, for men and women, faculty, staff, and students from varying racial, religious, and ethnic backgrounds, and of varying sexual orientations, as well as people with disabilities; and
4. Provide equal educational access to members of under-represented groups, and develop affirmative action admission programs where appropriate to achieve this goal.

Subd. 3. Promotion and Support. The University will promote and support diversity through its academic programs, its employment policies and practices, and the purchase of goods, materials, and services for its programs and facilities from businesses of the diverse communities it serves.

Subd. 4. Performance Goals. Administrative officers are directed to set performance goals consistent with this policy and the law, and energetically continue to implement the necessary programs and affirmative action administrative procedures for the achievement of these goals; to remedy any discriminatory practice which deviates from this policy; and to assess and reward the performance of individuals and units using the University's critical measures for the diversity performance goals as part of the University's planning and budgeting process. [http://www1.umn.edu/regents/policies/administrative/Diversity.html]

Religiously Affiliated Institution: The University of San Francisco

Equal Opportunity and Non-Discrimination Policy

The University is an equal opportunity institution of higher education. As a matter of policy, the University does not discriminate in employment, educational services and academic programs on the basis of an individual's race, color, religion, religious creed, ancestry, national origin, age (except minors), sex, sexual orientation, marital status, medical condition (cancer-related) and disability, and otherwise as required or permitted by law. The University reasonably accommodates qualified individuals with disabilities under the law.

[http://www.usfca.edu/acadserv/catalog/policies_equal_op.html]

References

Beemyn, B. "The Development and Administration of Campus LGBT Centers and Offices." In R. Sanlo, S. Rankin, and R. Schoenberg (eds.), *Our Place on Campus: Programs and Services for LGBT College Students.* Westport, Conn.: Greenwood Press, 2002.

Brown, S. "Are Gay Federal Workers Protected from Bias? Bush Appointee Wants to Change Policy." http://www.DiversityInc.com. Mar. 24, 2004. Accessed Jan. 4, 2005.

Cahill, S. "The Glass Nearly Half Full: 47% of U.S. Population Lives in Jurisdiction with Sexual Orientation Nondiscrimination Law." http://www.thetaskforce.org/downloads/GlassHalfFull.pdf. Jan. 5, 2005. Accessed Mar. 21, 2005.

Council for the Advancement of Standards in Higher Education (CAS). *Lesbian, Gay, Bisexual, and Transgender Programs and Services: Standards and Guidelines.* Washington, D.C.: CAS, 2001.

Dilley, P. "20th Century Postsecondary Practices and Policies to Control Gay Students." *Review of Higher Education,* 2002, 25(4), 409–431.

Henry J. Kaiser Family Foundation. *Inside-OUT: A Comprehensive Report on Lesbian, Gay and Bisexual Lives and Issues.* Menlo Park, Calif: Henry J. Kaiser Family Foundation, 2001.

Human Rights Campaign (HRC). http://www.hrc.org. Accessed Mar. 19, 2005.

Legal Definitions. http://www.legal-definitions.com. Accessed Mar. 29, 2005.

McNaron, T.A.H. *Poisoned Ivy: Lesbian and Gay Academics Confronting Homophobia.* Philadelphia: Temple University Press, 1996.

National Gay and Lesbian Task Force. "Coalition Against Discrimination in the Constitution." 2004. http://www.thetaskforce.org/reslibrary/list.cfm?pubTypeID=2# pub165. Accessed Mar. 21, 2005.

National Gay and Lesbian Task Force. "State Nondiscrimination Laws in the U.S." 2005a. http://www.thetaskforce.org/downloads/nondiscriminationmap.pdf. Accessed Mar. 21, 2005.

National Gay and Lesbian Task Force. "Anti–Gay Marriage Laws in the U.S." 2005b. http://www.thetaskforce.org/downloads/marriagemap.pdf. Accessed Mar. 21, 2005.

Raeburn, N. C. *Changing Corporate America Inside Out: Lesbian and Gay Workplace Rights*. Minneapolis: University of Minnesota Press, 2004.

Rankin, S. "The Campus Climate Report: Assessment and Intervention Strategies." In R. Sanlo (ed.), *Working with Lesbian, Gay, Bisexual, and Transgender College Students: A Handbook for Faculty and Administrators*. Westport, Conn.: Greenwood Press, 1998.

Sanlo, R. L. "The LGBT Campus Resource Center Director: The New Profession in Student Affairs." *NASPA Journal*, 2000, 37(3).

Shepard, C., Yeskel, F., and Outcalt, C. *Lesbian, Gay, Bisexual, and Transgender Campus Organizing: A Comprehensive Manual*. Washington, D.C.: National Gay and Lesbian Task Force, 1995.

Tobias, P. H., and Sauter, S. "Were You a Victim of Discrimination?" n.d. http://www.careerjournaleurope.com/myc/diversity/19971231-tobias.html. Accessed Mar. 29, 2005.

U.S. Equal Employment Opportunity Commission. http://www.eeoc.gov. Accessed Mar. 21, 2005.

Wrathall, J. D. "What Are You After? A History of Lesbians, Gay Men, Bisexuals, and Transgender People at the Twin Cities Campus at the University of Minnesota 1999–1993." In *Breaking the Silence: Final Report of the Select Committee on Lesbian, Gay, and Bisexual Concerns*. Minneapolis: University of Minnesota, 1993.

Yang, A. *From Wrongs to Rights: 1973 to 1999*. New York: National Gay and Lesbian Task Force, 1999.

Zemsky, B. "Coming Out of the Ivy Closet: Improving Campus Climate for LGBT Students, Staff, and Faculty." In W. Swan (ed.), *Handbook of Gay, Lesbian, and Transgender Administration and Policy*. New York: Marcel Dekker, 2004.

BETH ZEMSKY is coordinator of leadership and organizational effectiveness and faculty in LGBT Studies at the University of Minnesota. She is currently co-chair of the National Gay and Lesbian Task Force Board of Directors, and she was the founding director of the LGBT Programs Office at the University of Minnesota.

RONNI L. SANLO is director of the UCLA LGBT Campus Resource Center and a faculty in residence. She teaches in the UCLA Graduate School of Education.

2

Sexual minorities encounter unique challenges due to their sexual orientation, gender identity, or gender expression that often prevents them from achieving their full academic potential or participating fully in the campus community.

Campus Climates for Sexual Minorities

Susan R. Rankin

Sexual-minority students[1] on college or university campuses encounter unique challenges because of how they are perceived and treated as a result of their sexual orientation, gender identity, or gender expression. The challenges faced by gay, lesbian, bisexual, and transgender (LGBT) students can prevent them from achieving their full academic potential or participating fully in campus communities. Similarly, other LGBT faculty, staff, and administrators can suffer as a result of the same prejudices, which can limit their ability to achieve their career goals or to mentor or support students. This chapter examines current campus climates for lesbian, gay, and bisexual students and employees in institutions of higher education. *Campus climate* is defined here as the cumulative attitudes, behaviors, and standards of employees and students concerning access for, inclusion of, and level of respect for individual and group needs, abilities, and potential.

Literature Review

Several research articles (Brown, Clarke, Gortmaker, and Robinson-Keilig, 2004; Evans and Broido, 2002; Garber, 2002; Malaney, Williams, and Geller, 1997; Waldo, 1998) document the perceptions of campus quality of life for LGBT people. The results of these studies suggest that LGBT people are marginalized on campus. Additional research has documented the experiences of harassment and violence faced by LGBT people on campus (D'Augelli, 1992; Herek, 1993; Waldo, Hesson-McInnis, and D'Augelli, 1998) and the consequences of anti-LGBT harassment and violence on its victims (D'Augelli, 1992; Herek, 1994, 1995; Hershberger and D'Augelli, 1995; Norris and Kaniasty, 1991; Savin-Williams and Cohen, 1996; Slater,

New Directions for Student Services, no. 111, Fall 2005 © Wiley Periodicals, Inc.

1993). Still other research has examined the success of and best practices for programs to improve campus climate for LGBT people (Draughn, Elkins, and Roy, 2002; Little and Marx, 2002; Louvaas, Baroudi, and Collins, 2002; Sausa, 2002; Yep, 2002).

Some of this research focuses on perceptions of campus climate for sexual minorities. In these studies, LGBT college students generally rate campus climate lower than their non-LGBT peers (Brown, Clarke, Gortmaker, and Robinson-Keilig, 2004; Waldo, 1998). Rankin (1998) noted that LGBT students are targeted for harassment and violence more often than non-LGBT students; derogatory comments were noted as the most common form of harassment.

Another body of literature suggests several predictors of positive attitudes toward LGBT people. These include knowing someone who is LGBT (Malaney, Williams, and Geller, 1997; Norris and Kaniasty, 1991), being comfortable with one's own sexual identity (Simoni, 1996), being female (Engstrom and Sedlacek, 1997), and not being a first-year student (Brown, Clarke, Gortmaker, and Robinson-Keilig, 2004; Engstrom and Sedlaceck, 1997; Malaney, Williams, and Geller, 1997). This research also suggests that resident assistants and other student affairs staff members are more sensitive to the issues and concerns of LGBT students than members of the general student or staff population and faculty (Brown, Clarke, Gortmaker, and Robinson-Keilig, 2004).

The Rankin Study

The studies referred to were all conducted at one or two institutions or within one department at one institution. In an effort to examine the climate for LGBT people at a national level, I designed a study to examine the experiences of LGBT people, their perceptions of campus climate for LGBT people, and their perceptions of institutional responses to LGBT issues and concerns (Rankin, 2003). Fourteen campuses participated in the study: four private and ten public colleges and universities from across the country. The respondent sample (1,669 self-identified LGBT people) is larger than that of any other study using one assessment tool.[2]

The results of my study indicated that more than one-third (36 percent) of LGBT undergraduate students have experienced harassment within the past year (Table 2.1). Derogatory remarks were the most common form of harassment (89 percent). Other types of harassment included spoken harassment or threats (48 percent), anti-LGBT graffiti (39 percent), pressure to conceal one's sexual orientation or gender identity (38 percent), written comments (33 percent), and physical assaults (reported by eleven respondents). Seventy-nine percent of those harassed identified students as the source of the harassment. Of the eleven physical assaults noted in the study, ten were reported by students. These findings point to the need for intervention strategies aimed at student populations on campus.

Table 2.1. Harassment Experienced by LGBT Students and Staff, Rankin Study

Experienced Harassment?	Undergraduate Student % (n)	Graduate/Professional Student % (n)	Staff % (n)	Faculty % (n)	Administrator % (n)
Yes	36 (254)	23 (63)	19 (72)	27 (41)	32 (30)
No	64 (459)	77 (216)	81 (299)	73 (109)	68 (65)

Table 2.2. Perceptions of Harassment Toward LGBT People

Perceptions of Harassment Toward:	Very Unlikely % (n)	Somewhat Likely % (n)	Uncertain % (n)	Somewhat Likely % (n)	Very Likely % (n)
Gay men	3 (41)	13 (219)	22 (369)	41 (690)	19 (324)
Lesbians	4 (67)	18 (298)	23 (388)	42 (693)	12 (196)
Bisexual people	5 (87)	19 (311)	37 (609)	28 (471)	10 (163)
Transgender people	2 (31)	4 (70)	21 (348)	29 (486)	42 (702)

The results also indicated that 20 percent of the respondents feared for their physical safety because of their sexual orientation or gender identity, and 51 percent concealed their sexual orientation or gender identity to avoid intimidation. In addition, respondents in the study felt that LGBT people were likely to be harassed on campus.

Moreover, most faculty (73 percent), students (74 percent), administrators (81 percent), and staff (73 percent) described their campus climates for LGBT people as homophobic. In contrast, most respondents perceived the campus climates for non-LGBT people as friendly (90 percent), concerned (75 percent), and respectful (80 percent). Both the perceived and experienced harassment LGBT people noted in the literature discussed earlier support this finding (Table 2.2).

Forty-one percent of the respondents stated that their college or university did not thoroughly address issues related to sexual orientation or gender identity. This view was strongest among administrators (44 percent), gay individuals (46 percent), and transgender people (42 percent). Further, 43 percent of the participants felt that the curriculum did not represent the contributions of LGBT people (Table 2.3).

This research also suggests that LGBT people of color were more likely than white LGBT people to conceal their sexual orientation or gender identity to avoid harassment. Many respondents commented in the open-ended portion of the study that they did not feel comfortable being "out" (open

Table 2.3. Response of Institution and Curriculum to Issues of Sexual Orientation and Gender Identity

Institutional Response	Strongly Agree % (n)	Agree % (n)	Uncertain % (n)	Disagree % (n)	Strongly Disagree % (n)
The college/university thoroughly addresses campus issues related to sexual orientation/ gender identity	6 (101)	31 (515)	21 (350)	29 (482)	12 (199)
The curriculum adequately represents the contributions of LGBT persons	4 (63)	18 (300)	34 (568)	29 (480)	14 (233)

about their sexual-minority status) in venues where straight people of color were predominant and felt out of place in predominantly white LGBT settings. Also, although nontransgender LGB men and women (28 percent) reported experiencing harassment, a significantly higher proportion of transgender respondents (41 percent) reported experiences of harassment.

Institutional Responses and Actions

The research from the past two decades demonstrates that college campuses have been inhospitable, and even hostile, toward their LGBT members. To address this concern, several institutions have initiated structural changes, such as creating LGBT resource centers and safe-space programs, and provided institutional recognition to LGBT student groups. In addition, many have revised or created LGBT-inclusive practices, such as domestic partner benefits or nondiscrimination policies. Others have launched LGBT-inclusive educational initiatives in staff orientations and sensitivity trainings for resident assistants and have integrated LGBT issues into curricula (National Consortium of Directors of LGBT Resources in Higher Education, 2004). Yet, even on some of these campuses the climate reported by members of the LGBT community in my 2003 study was less than welcoming.

That study examined the climate on campuses that had designed proactive initiatives such as those described to address the particular needs and vulnerabilities of LGBT people. The results suggested that despite those initiatives, LGBT people fear for their safety, keep their identities secret, experience harassment, and feel that their universities are unsupportive of LGBT people. If these are the experiences and perceptions on these "proactive" campuses, colleges without such initiatives may leave LGBT people feeling even more afraid, vulnerable, and less supported. The realities of these lives must be addressed through the creation of programs to lower rates of harassment and violence and assure LGBT people that the university is a truly safe and supportive place where they, like other members of the academic community, can reach their full potential as workers and learners.

The research on the needs of LGBT people suggests that these interventions fall into three categories: institutional support and commitment to an LGBT-friendly campus; recruitment and retention of open LGBT students, faculty, and staff; and attention to LGBT student life, including social outlets, housing, and safety (Windmeyer and Rankin, n.d.). Examples of best practices in these types of programs include "safe zone" programs (Draughn, Elkins, and Roy, 2002), the inclusion of LGBT people in the mainstream curricula and the creation of curricula focused on the study of LGBT people, creation of residence life centers or resource centers focused on LGBT needs and issues (Herbst and Malaney, 1999), creation and implementation of antidiscrimination policies, and the creation and implementation of rapid response systems to record and address the needs of students who have experienced violence and harassment on campus (for overviews of existing programs for LGBT students, see also Garber, 2002; National Consortium of Directors of LGBT Resources in Higher Education, 2004; Rankin, 2003).

Future Directions

This chapter examined the climate on campus for LGBT people. The review revealed that many LGBT people on campus hide significant parts of their identity from peers and others, thereby isolating themselves socially or emotionally. Those who do not hide their sexual-minority identity have a range of experiences, including discrimination, verbal or physical harassment, and subtle or outright silencing of their sexual identities.

Although individual programs or interventions (that is, LGBT centers, LGBT policy inclusion, and so forth) are important because they provide needed services to LGBT people and demonstrate institutional support, the "paradigm shift" in treatment of LGBT people and recognition of their concerns called for by Schreier (1995) demands more than individual programs or enforced tolerance of LGBT people.

As participants in institutions of power, higher education faculty and staff are part of systems of relations that can silence those who are not in positions of power. Heterosexism and homophobia, for example, operate to reinforce the heterosexual norm. Differences disturb the norm; a culture of silence reinforces the norm for those who are different. When LGBT people on campus increase their visibility and, therefore, their voice on campus, they challenge heterosexual norms. By providing a voice through visible LGBT-supportive initiatives on campus, they engage in dialogue and action with individuals who may have different ideas and perceptions about the world. This is hard work, but such work creates the conditions for change.

To address the challenges facing LGBT people on campus successfully, a shift of basic assumptions, premises, and beliefs must take place in all areas of the institution; only then can behavior and structures be changed. In the transformed institution, heterosexist assumptions are replaced by assumptions of diverse sexualities and relationships, and these new assumptions govern the design and implementation of all institutional activities, programs, and services. Transformative change demands committed leadership in articulating both institutional goals and policies. New approaches to learning, teaching, decision making, and working in the institution are implemented.

New approaches to creating transformative change include creating centers for interdisciplinary study and cross-cultural teaching and learning inclusive of LGBT issues; supporting active, collaborative learning concerned with helping students to come to grips with their identities; and reconfiguring classes by encouraging students to assist in developing or changing the syllabus at the start of and during the semester.

Notes

1. The author acknowledges the personal and political import of language and the need to recognize a broad range of self-identity choices. This chapter uses the terms *sexual minorities* and *lesbian, gay, bisexual, and transgender (LGBT)* when referring to sexual orientation, gender identity, or gender expression. Many individuals identified as LGBT may choose to use other self-identifying terms or none at all.
2. Despite the large sample size, caution must be used when attempting to generalize from the results to all institutions of higher education. The institutions that agreed to participate in this study all had a visible LGBT presence on campus (for example, a resource center with a paid staff person who had at least part-time responsibilities to address LGBT concerns on campus), whereas nationwide fewer than one hundred institutions of higher education have such resources.

References

Brown, R., Clarke, B., Gortmaker, V., and Robinson-Keilig, R. "Assessing the Campus Climate for Gay, Lesbian, Bisexual and Transgender (LGBT) Students Using a Multiple Perspectives Approach." *Journal of College Student Development,* 2004, *45*(1), 8–26.

D'Augelli, A. "Lesbian and Gay Male Undergraduates' Experiences of Harassment and Fear on Campus." *Journal of Interpersonal Violence,* 1992, 7(3), 383–395.

Draughn, T., Elkins, B., and Roy, R. "Allies in the Struggle: Eradicating Homophobia and Heterosexism on Campus." *Journal of Lesbian Studies,* 2002, 6(3/4), 9–20.

Engstrom, C., and Sedlacek, W. "Attitudes of Heterosexual Students Toward Their Gay and Lesbian Peers." *Journal of College Student Development,* 1997, 38(6), 565–577.

Evans, N., and Broido, E. "The Experiences of Lesbian and Bisexual Women." *Journal of Lesbian Studies,* 2002, 6(3/4), 29–40.

Garber, L. "Weaving a Wide Net: The Benefits of Integrating Campus Projects to Combat Homophobia." *Journal of Lesbian Studies,* 2002, 6(3/4), 21–28.

Herek, G. "Documenting Prejudice Against Lesbians and Gay Men: The Yale Sexual Orientation Study." *Journal of Homosexuality,* 1993, 25(4), 15–30.

Herek, G. "Heterosexism, Hate Crimes, and the Law." In M. Costanzo and S. Oskamp (eds.), *Violence and the Law.* Newberry Park, Calif.: Sage, 1994.

Herbst, S., and Malaney, G. D. "Perceived Value of a Special Interest Residential Program for Gay, Lesbian, Bisexual, and Transgender Students." *NASPA Journal,* 1999, 36(2), 106–119.

Herek, G. "Psychological Heterosexism in the United States." In A. R. D'Augelli and C. J. Paterson (eds.), *Lesbian, Gay and Bisexual Identities Across the Lifespan.* New York: Oxford University Press, 1995.

Hershberger, S. L., and D'Augelli, A. R. "The Impact of Victimization on the Mental Health and Suicidality of Lesbian, Gay and Bisexual Youth." *Developmental Psychology,* 1995, *31,* 65–74.

Little, P., and Marx, M. "Teaching About Heterosexism and Creating an Empathic Experience of Homophobia." *Journal of Lesbian Studies,* 2002, *6*(3/4), 205–218.

Louvaas, K., Baroudi, L., and Collins, S. "*Transcending* Heteronormativity in the Classroom: Using Queer and Critical Pedagogies to Alleviate Trans-Anxieties." *Journal of Lesbian Studies,* 2002, *6*(3/4), 177–189.

Malaney, G., Williams, E., and Geller, W. "Assessing Campus Climate for Gays, Lesbians and Bisexuals at Two Institutions." *Journal of College Student Development,* 1997, *38*(4), 356–375.

National Consortium of Directors of LGBT Resources in Higher Education. 2004. http://www.lgbtcampus.org/directory.htm. Accessed Mar. 25, 2005.

Norris, F. H., and Kaniasty, K. "The Psychological Experience of Crime: A Test of the Mediating Role of Beliefs in Explaining the Distress of Victims." *Journal of Social and Clinical Psychology,* 1991, *10,* 239–261.

Rankin, S. "The Campus Climate Report: Assessment and Intervention Strategies." In R. Sanlo (ed.), *Working with Lesbian, Gay, Bisexual, and Transgender College Students: A Handbook for Faculty and Administrators.* Westport, Conn.: Greenwood Press, 1998.

Rankin, S. *Campus Climate for LGBT People: A National Perspective.* New York: National Gay and Lesbian Task Force Policy Institute, 2003.

Sausa, L. "Updating College and University Campus Policies: Meeting the Needs of Trans Students, Staff and Faculty." *Journal of Lesbian Studies,* 2002, *6*(3/4), 43–55.

Savin-Williams, R. C., and Cohen, M. N. (eds.). *The Lives of Lesbians, Gays and Bisexuals: Children to Adults.* Fort Worth: Harcourt Brace, 1996.

Schreier, B. "Moving Beyond Tolerance: A New Paradigm for Programming About Homophoba/Biphobia and Heterosexism." *Journal of College Student Development,* 1995, *36*(1), 19–26.

Simoni, J. "Pathways to Prejudice: Predicting Students' Heterosexist Attitudes with Demographics, Self-Esteem and Contact with Lesbians and Gay Men." *Journal of College Student Development,* 1996, *37*(1), 68–77.

Slater, B. "Violence Against Lesbians and Gay Male College Students." *Journal of College Student Psychotherapy,* 1993, *8*(1/2), 177–202.

Waldo, C. "Out on Campus: Sexual Orientation and Academic Climate in a University Context." *American Journal of Community Psychology,* 1998, *26*(5), 745–774.

Waldo, C., Hesson-McInnis, M., and D'Augelli, A. "Antecedents and Consequences of Victimization of Lesbian, Gay and Bisexual Young People: A Structural Model Comparing Rural University and Urban Samples." *American Journal of Community Psychology,* 1998, *26*(2), 307–334.

Windmeyer, S., and Rankin, S. "Best LGBT Colleges and Universities." n.d. Unpublished paper.

Yep, G. "From Homophobia and Heterosexism to Heteronormativity: Toward the Development of a Model of Queer Interventions in the University Classroom." *Journal of Lesbian Studies,* 2002, *6*(3/4), 163–176.

SUSAN R. RANKIN is senior diversity planning analyst and assistant professor of higher education at Pennsylvania State University.

3

A review of LGBT identity development models reveals fluidity, complexity, and contradictions.

Analysis of LGBT Identity Development Models and Implications for Practice

Brent L. Bilodeau, Kristen A. Renn

In their efforts to serve all students more effectively, many student affairs professionals seek to understand how students come to have and enact lesbian, gay, bisexual, and transgender (LGBT) identities. In the past two decades, student affairs professionals have adopted psychosocial models of sexual orientation identity development (Cass, 1979, 1984), and a handful of scholars (D'Augelli, 1994; Evans and Broido, 1999; Rhoads, 1994) have attempted to describe LGBT identity in higher education settings. This chapter presents an overview of literature regarding models of LGBT identity development, including stage models of sexual orientation identity development, theories specific to LGBT people of color, a life span approach to LGBT identity development, and approaches to transgender identity development. Thematic similarities and differences as well as implications for educational practice and research are discussed.

Stage Models of Gay and Lesbian Identity Development

In the United States, the 1970s marked a new era in research regarding sexual orientation identity development with the emergence of theoretical stage models describing homosexual identity. These models focused on the resolution of internal conflict related to identification as lesbian or gay, and informed what is commonly termed the *coming-out* process (see, for example, Cass, 1979, 1984; Fassinger, 1991; Savin-Williams, 1988, 1990; Troiden, 1979, 1988). Based on studies with small sample sizes, most often of men, these theoretical perspectives assert that non-heterosexuals move through a series of identity development stages, usually during the teenage years or early twenties. Though the number of stages and their names vary across theories, they share common characteristics. Gonsiorek (1995) described shared aspects of these models as follows.

Typically, these models begin with a stage in which individuals use multiple defense strategies to block recognition of personal homosexual feelings. These defensive strategies are maintained for an unspecified time period in an attempt to minimize an individual's same-gender feelings. The process of expending energy to deny and minimize feelings may have negative consequences for overall emotional health. Yet, for many individuals, a gradual recognition and tentative acceptance of same-gender feelings emerge as they come to accept that their feelings are not heterosexually oriented. According to the stage models, this emergence of same-gender feelings is followed by a period of emotional and behavioral experimentation with homosexuality, often accompanied by a growing sense of personal normality. Some models describe the ending of a first relationship as a time of identity crisis in which negative feelings about being gay or lesbian return. As the individual again begins to accept non-heterosexual feelings, a sense of identity as lesbian or gay becomes internally integrated and is viewed as a positive aspect of self. While most scholars describe the coming-out process in clear stages, they also note that it is generally more fluid, with stops, starts, and backtracking (Cass, 1979, 1984; Troiden, 1979; Savin-Williams, 1990).

Differences among the stage models illustrate the difficulty of using only one model to understand a complex psychosocial process (the development of sexual orientation identity). Yet, the predominance and persistence of stage models in the research literature and in current educational practice suggest that they represent with some accuracy the developmental process. In contrast, Ryan and Futterman (1998) noted that most of lesbian, gay, and bisexual identity development models were based on research on adults reflecting on their experience. Few models exist that specifically address developmental issues of lesbian, gay, and bisexual adolescents.

Adolescence and Sexual Orientation Identity Development

Research on adolescents and sexual orientation supplements the stage models with information specific to youth and college students. Research on teenage youth notes a trend in which self-identification as lesbian, gay, or bisexual happens at increasingly earlier ages (Troiden, 1998). It is therefore more likely that students will enter college having already begun—or completed—the coming-out process.

When considering developmental issues of adolescents and sexual orientation, it is also important to note that these years may be characterized by sexual experimentation as well as by confusion about identity (Ryan and Futterman, 1998; Savin-Williams, 1990). Same-gender adolescent sexual experiences do not necessarily signal a lesbian, gay, or bisexual identity (Blumenfeld and Raymond, 1993). Conversely, adolescents may identify as lesbian, gay, or bisexual without having had any sexual experience (Ryan and Futterman, 1998; Savin-Williams, 1990). The diversity of individual adolescents' experiences of identifying as lesbian, gay, or bisexual highlights the need to consider multiple developmental models.

Research on LGBT Identities in Bisexuals, People of Color, and Women

There is growing scholarly recognition of the experience and diversity of sexual orientation beyond "heterosexual," "gay," and "lesbian" identities, and this recognition has led to challenges to the traditional stage models of sexual orientation identity development. Scholars have found that bisexuals experience identity processes differently from the way lesbians and gay men do (Fox, 1995; Klein, 1990, 1993). For example, some individuals may come to bisexual identity after self-labeling as lesbian or gay. Others may identify bisexual feelings from childhood onward. Still others may not become aware of bisexual feelings until after experiencing heterosexual relationships or marriages. Further, stage models do not account for ways in which the boundaries between Eurocentric notions of culture, sexual orientation, and gender identity are blurred and reconstructed in non-Western contexts (Brown, 1997; Gonsiorek, 1995). One such example is the existence of "Two Spirit" identities that blend Western notions of gender identity and sexual orientation within Native American communities (Brown, 1997). Across cultures, LGBT identities have different names and meanings.

Researchers are providing new perspectives on the experience of multiple and intersecting identities related to race and ethnicity, nationality, and sexuality. Research regarding the ways race and culture interact with the experience of LGBT identities in the United States has expanded (Boykin, 1996, on African Americans; Diaz, 1997, and Espin, 1993, on Latinos; Manalansan, 1993, on Asian Americans; Crow, Brown, and Wright, 1997, and Wilson, 1996, on Native Americans). Beyond the United States, scholarship on the intersections of LGBT identities and nationality is expanding as well, particularly in reference to Africans, Latin Americans, Middle Easterners, and South and East Asians (Ben-Ari, 2001; Kapack, 1992; Kovac, 2002; McLelland, 2000).

Additional research addresses the influence of gender, socioeconomic class, ability, and spirituality on LGBT identity development. Regarding gender differences, women's non-heterosexual identity processes have most often been presented as paralleling those of men, yet a number of scholars indicate that women may come out and have intimate same-gender experiences at somewhat later ages (Brown, 1995; Sears, 1989). Recent research explores LGBT identities related to social class and class systems, posing questions about how non-heterosexual identities intersect with class privilege and oppression (Becker, 1997; Raffo, 1997; Vanderbosh, 1997). Scholarship is emerging that addresses ways that identities of people with disabilities are influenced by LGBT identity processes (Clare, 1999). DuMontier (2000) hypothesized interactions between sexual orientation and faith development, and other authors discuss specific religious traditions and sexual orientation identity (Love, 1998).

By expanding the theoretical bases for understanding LGBT identities beyond those represented by white, Western men in the foundational models of homosexual identity formation (such as Cass, 1979 and 1984, and Troiden, 1979), researchers provide a complex picture of non-heterosexual identity. They highlight the social context of non-heterosexual identities across cultures and draw attention to the diversity that exists within LGBT communities.

Alternatives to Stage Models: A Life Span Approach to Sexual Orientation and Gender Identity Development

As more scholars describe the development of non-heterosexual identity as a fluid and complex process influenced by other psychosocial identities, it becomes apparent that stage models are not adequate to describe all non-heterosexual identity processes. In addition, bisexual and transgender experiences, with their emphasis on identities existing outside traditional binary constructions of gender and sexuality, pose unique challenges to stage models. Though no identity development model can fully address the intersections and complexities of non-heterosexual identity, D'Augelli (1994) offered a "life span" model of sexual orientation development that takes social contexts into account in ways that the early stage models did not. As well, D'Augelli's model has the potential to represent a wider range of experiences than the theories relating to specific racial, ethnic, or gender groups.

The D'Augelli framework addresses issues often ignored in other models, presenting human development as unfolding in concurring and multiple paths, including the development of a person's self-concept, relationships with family, and connections to peer groups and community. This model suggests that sexual orientation may be very fluid at certain times in the life span and more fixed at others and that human growth is intimately connected to and shaped by environmental and biological factors. The D'Augelli model describes six "identity processes" that operate more or less independently and are not ordered in stages:

- Exiting heterosexuality
- Developing a personal LGB identity
- Developing an LGB social identity

- Becoming an LGB offspring
- Developing an LGB intimacy status
- Entering an LGB community

An individual may experience development in one process to a greater extent than another; for example, he or she may have a strong LGB social identity and an intimate same-sex partner, but not have come out as LGB to family (become an LGB offspring). Furthermore, depending on the context and timing, he or she may be at different points of development in a given process, such as when an openly LGB person enters a new work setting and chooses not to express his or her LGB identity.

Developed to represent sexual orientation identity development, D'Augelli's model has also been used for understanding corresponding processes in the formation of transgender identity (Renn and Bilodeau, 2005). In a recent study of transgender identity development in college students, Bilodeau (2005) noted that participants described their gender identies in ways that reflect the six processes of the D'Augelli model. Research on transgender college students is rare, and differences between sexual orientation and gender identity are not always well understood (Bilodeau, 2005).

Definitions of Transgender Identities

The term *gender identity* has been used to describe an individual's internal sense of self as male, female, or an identity between or outside these two categories (Wilchins, 2002). Individuals whose biological sex assignment matches male or female gender identity and the range of related behavioral expressions deemed acceptable by societal norms may be referred to as "traditionally gendered." The term *transgender* focuses on individuals whose gender identity conflicts with biological sex assignment or societal expectations for gender expression as male or female (Bornstein, 1994; Elkins and King, 1996; Wilchins, 1997, 2002).

The term *transgender* is often used as an inclusive category for a wide range of identities, including transsexuals, transvestites, male and female impersonators, drag kings and queens, male-to-female (MTF) persons, female-to-male (FTM) persons, cross-dressers, gender benders, gender variant, gender nonconforming, and ambiguously gendered persons (Bornstein, 1994; Feinberg, 1996; O'Keefe and Fox, 1997; Wilchins, 1997, 2002). While these terms are more commonly used in the United States, it is important to note that in a number of non-Western societies, transgender identities are defined with a unique terminology reflecting cultural norms (Besnier, 1993; Brown, 1997; Johnson, 1997). In these contexts, gender identity and sexual orientation are presented as more integrated identities, compared with the Western medical and psychiatric tradition of segmenting sexual orientation and gender identity into distinctive categories.

Western Psychiatric and Medical Perspectives on Transgender Identities

As Western psychiatric and medical traditions have set the standards for the diagnosis and care of transgender persons in the United States, it is important to consider their impact. While various scholars, as well as members of the transgender community, regard these traditions as invaluable for addressing the needs of transgender persons (Brown and Rounsley, 1996), others suggest that medical and psychiatric perspectives are dominated by themes of transgender identities as forms of mental illness and biological malady (Califia, 1997). The term *disorder* dominates the literature. Medical and psychiatric literature focuses primarily on a binary construction of transgender identity (all individuals should be assigned to either male or female categories), with an emphasis on "correcting" gender deviance through reassignment to the "appropriate" gender. This focus makes transsexuals—individuals who often choose to transition from one gender to another with medical assistance—of primary concern.

A section on Gender Identity Disorder (GID) appears for the first time in the American Psychiatric Association's 1980 publication, *Diagnostic and Statistical Manual of Mental Disorders, 3rd Edition (DSM-III)*. GID is described as incongruence between biological sex assignment and gender identity. Three different types of GID diagnoses are discussed: transsexualism, non-transsexualism type, and not otherwise specified (American Psychiatric Association, 1980). In *DSM III*, treatments described vary from psychotherapy to sex reassignment surgery (SRS). Three more editions of DSM have appeared since 1980.

The current edition, *Diagnostic and Statistical Manual of Mental Disorders, 4th Edition, Text Revision (DSM-IV-TR)* (American Psychiatric Association, 2000), continues the use of the GID classification, but expands diagnosis standards introduced in *DSM-III*. In *DSM-IV-TR*, there are four major criteria that must be present to make a diagnosis. First, there must be evidence of a strong and persistent cross-gender identification, which is the desire to be, or the insistence that one is, of the other gender (Criteria A). This cross-gender identification must not merely be a desire for any perceived cultural advantages of being the other gender. Second, there must also be evidence of persistent discomfort about one's assigned gender (based on biological anatomy) or a sense of inappropriateness in the gender role of that assigned gender (Criteria B). Third, the individual must not have a concurrent physical intersex condition (referring to conditions in which a person is born with a reproductive or sexual anatomy that does not fit the typical definitions of female or male) (Criteria C). Fourth, there must be evidence of clinically significant distress or impairment in social, occupational, or other important areas of functioning (Criteria D). In the case of transsexuality, individuals are further categorized under primary transsexualism (emerging in early childhood) or secondary transsexualism (emerging during or after puberty). GID is used primarily to diagnose conditions related to transsexual identities, while another classification, Gender Identity Disorder Not Otherwise Specified (GIDNOS), applies to conditions such as intersex anatomy or cross-dressing behavior (American Psychiatric Association, 2000).

DSM-IV-TR is complemented by the fifth edition of the *Harry Benjamin Standards of Care for Gender Identity Disorders*, which outlined a treatment framework, including therapeutic and medical guidelines, as well as standards for ongoing evaluation of patients who are undergoing sex reassignment surgery (Harry Benjamin International Gender Dysphoria Association, 2001). A number of scholars (including Bornstein, 1994; Carter, 2000; Mallon, 1999b) are highly critical of *DSM-IV-TR* and the Harry Benjamin Standards of Care, citing their negative, stigmatizing nature. Using these two frameworks, an individual must in essence be documented as having a mental illness (using *DSM-IV-TR)* in order to access sex reassignment surgery (as specified by the Harry Benjamin Standards of Care) (Carter, 2000).

Literature consistently identifies a growing outrage in transgender communities regarding the GID diagnosis (see Califia, 1997; Carter, 2000; Wilchins, 2002). Pressure to remove gender identity disorders from *DSM-VI-TR* has been compared to the 1973 removal of homosexuality as a mental illness diagnostic classification from the 1973 edition of the *DSM* (Carter, 2000). Pauline Parks, a transgender activist, argues that every psychiatrist who diagnoses GID in a patient merely by virtue of the individual's transgender identity is complicit in the manipulation and control of transgender people and their bodies. Parks asserts that in diagnosing someone with a so-called illness that the person does not have, the psychiatrist engages in behavior that not only is unethical, but also constitutes medical malpractice (Cooper, 1999).

Further, medical and psychiatric literature focuses primarily on a binary construction of gender identity. Normality is defined as a biological and gender identity match as either male or female. The majority of medical and therapeutic approaches are designed to assist individuals in moving from one gender to another. These approaches do not fully address the needs of individuals who, for a variety of reasons, may forgo gender reassignment surgery or may define gender identity as existing outside binary notions of male or female identities. In reaction to binary identities, one transgender college student described self as follows:

> I'd use the word transgender. I'd also use "non-operational female to male." I'd also use the word "genderqueer." I identified as a feminist before identifying as trans. It was really embedded in me. It played a big part in my decision not to have surgery. I've tried with my identity to not reinforce the gender binary system, and options have been limited to the trans community by focusing so much on transsexualism (involving gender reassignment surgery). The only option is, if you're male, to become female, or vice-versa. Transgender youth have felt that binary gender system is not for them. We want to increase the number of genders. [Bilodeau, 2005]

Though medical and psychiatric approaches comprise the dominant paradigm for addressing the concerns and needs of transgender persons in the United States, it is apparent that these perspectives provide only partial understanding of the range of ways transgender identities are expressed.

Feminist, Postmodern, and Queer Theory Perspectives on Gender Identity

Feminist, postmodern, and queer theoretical scholars present significant alternatives to medical and psychiatric perspectives on gender identity. A number of these scholars suggest that gender identity is not necessarily linked to biological sex assignment at birth, but is created through complex social interactions and influenced by the dynamics of institutionalized power inequalities (Butler, 1990, 1993; Halberstam, 1998; Wilchins, 2002). Further, this framework takes issue with binary male or female constructions of gender and transgender expression as mental illness, favoring more fluid notions of gender identity (Butler, 1990, 1993; Creed, 1995; Feinberg, 1996, 1998; Halberstam, 1998, Wilchins, 2002). Regarding systemic power and gender, Bornstein (1994) suggested that gender is essentially a binary, male or female class system. This system leads to negation of the existence of more fluid gender identities increasingly expressed by transgender youth (Bilodeau, forthcoming; Wilchins, 2002). The systemic privileging of the binary, two-gender system has been described by the term *genderism* (Wilchins, 2002).

As alternatives to binary gender identity constructions and related oppressive systems, a number of feminist, postmodern, and queer theorists posit transgender identities and gender fluidity as normative and cite as evidence centuries of global traditions of gender-nonconforming identities (Butler, 1990, 1993; Creed, 1995; Feinberg, 1996, 1998; Halberstam, 1998). As examples, Feinberg (1996) documented several instances in Western European history where gender variance and transgression existed, including Joan of Arc, Amelia Earhart, and Rebecca's Daughters (cross-dressing Welsh resistance fighters in World War II). Beyond normalizing support of transgender identities, a number of feminist, postmodern, and queer theorists suggest that all individuals may benefit from the dismantling of dual gender systems, promoting greater freedom from rigid gender roles (Feinberg, 1996; Wilchins, 2002). Themes reflecting these perspectives are also emerging in human development spheres.

Human Development and Transgender Identities: A Call for New Theoretical Models

A notable contribution in the human development field is the volume *Social Services with Transgendered Youth* (Mallon, 1999a), which primarily focuses on adolescent populations. In particular, the book addresses problematic issues of *DSM-IV* and broadens attention to ways youth construct gender identity outside binary systems. In another publication, Mallon (1999b) argued that it is inappropriate for social service practitioners to use traditional human development models, including those of Erikson (1950) and Marcia (1980), because these theorists posit concepts of gender role identification in traditionally gendered, biologically based constructions. Though an increasing number of studies of transgender persons are emerging (Denny, 1998; Devor, 1997), Mallon (1999b) suggested that this work has yet to propose the creation of healthy, nonstigmatizing models of transgender identity development. He calls upon human service practitioners to create such models and to develop an in-depth understanding of cross-disciplinary trends regarding sexual orientation and gender identity concerns.

Multiple Perspectives Related to Sexual Orientation and Gender Identity

To summarize the theoretical lenses presented in this chapter, models and theories related to sexual orientation and gender identity development differ in scope, format, and underlying epistemological assumptions. These perspectives range from being based on assumptions of a universal linear experience of identity development to relying more on the social context of the developing person. Some models assume that sexual orientation and gender identity have distinctive natures, separate from the interplay of identity characteristics related to race, nationality, disability, spirituality, and socioeconomic class. Other models view diverse identity characteristics as inextricably linked to the development and expression of sexual orientation and gender identity. In addition, some models assume an essentialized, biologically determined nature of sexual orientation and gender identity, while others focus on the social construction of identity. These assumptions, as well as the nature of the research sample (if any) on which the model was based, influence the general characteristics of families of theories. Table 3.1 summarizes some of these characteristics, origins, strengths, and criticisms.

Implications for Student Affairs Practice and Scholarship

The choice of a particular theoretical model influences educational practice and research. Practitioners and scholars must take into account the value-laden nature of theories related to sexual orientation and gender identity development. As an example, a worthy student affairs goal is to support LGBT students in ongoing self-work surrounding personal identity. Basing educational interventions intended to promote development on linear models, however, may imply that there is an ideal endpoint that students should be prompted to attain. The educational initiative could imply that to be at any stage other than the endpoint is inferior.

Table 3.1. Comparison of Sexual Orientation and Gender Identity Development Theories

	Stage Models of Sexual Orientation Identity Development	Life Span and Other Nonlinear Models of Sexual Orientation Identity Development	Diverse Perspectives on Sexual Orientation and Gender Identity	Medical and Psychiatric Perspectives on Gender Identity	Feminist, Postmodern and Queer Perspectives on Gender Identity
Examples of Theorists or Sources	Cass, Fassinger, Savin-Williams, Troiden	D'Augelli, Fox, Klein, Rhoads	Boykin, L. S. Brown, Clare, Diaz, Raffo, Wilson	Diagnostic and Statistical Manual of Mental Disorders, Fourth Edition, Text Revision; Harry Benjamin Standards of Care	Butler, Creed, Feinberg, Halberstam, Wilchins
General characteristics of models	Linear progression from lack of awareness of sexual orientation through immersion in identity to integration of identity.	Focus on specific processes of identity development within sociocultural and life span context.	Describe LGBT identity and development in relation to other psychosocial identities (gender, race, culture, class, ability, and so on).	Posit "normal" gender identity as that in which gender identity corresponds in traditional ways to biological sex; transgenderism and transsexuality are viewed as psychiatric disorders.	Posit gender identity as socially constructed within system of power based on gender, race, class, sexual orientation, ability, and other socially constructed categories.
Samples on which models were based	General adult population, clinical or incarcerated populations (Cass)	College students, general adult population	Subpopulations of adults, adolescents, college students	Clinical populations	None; scholarship and theories not typically derived from empirical research

Strengths of these models for higher education practice	—Offer parallel theories of human development (such as Erikson, 1950) in progression from less to more complex ways of understanding self and society —Conceptualize development in a way that can be understood and applied in campus settings	—Account for context of identity development —Illuminate processes as well as outcomes of identity development —Some were developed specific to college context	—Enrich theoretical basis for understanding LGBT identity in multicultural contexts —Challenge universalized notions of LGBT identity —Support development of programs and services that meet needs of diverse student populations	—Provide legal basis for provision of services to transgender individuals under the Americans with Disabilities Act	—Account for context of identity development —Illuminate psychosocial elements of college environment that may influence gender identity —Account for structural differences in power —Do not provide theoretical background on identity development per se —Most are not specific to college environment or experience
Criticisms of these models	—Appear to prescribe a universal linear developmental trajectory that does not fit the experience of many individuals —Imply an endpoint and appear to value achievement of that endpoint as most healthy outcome of identity development —Ignore individual differences (gender, race, class, culture, and so on) that may influence or interact with sexual orientation identity —Many are not specific to college environment or experience —Many were developed with small empirical samples or were not based on empirical data	—Many are not specific to college environment or experience —Many were developed with small empirical samples or were not based on empirical data	—Some appear to assume fixed notions of socially constructed categories (gender, race, class, and so on) and universality of experience of LGBT people within those categories —Many were developed with small empirical samples or were not based on empirical data —Many are not specific to college environment or experience	—Appear to ignore social contexts of gender identity development and enactment —Tend to pathologize as mentally ill individuals whose gender identity does not conform to their biological sex —Most are not specific to college environment or experience —Ignore individual differences (race, class, culture, and so on) that may influence or interact with gender identity	

Alternatively, if the theoretical family selected as the basis to design LGBT student support initiatives is feminist, postmodern, or queer, design considerations should address the social construction of LGBT identities within systems of campus power. Example questions and related issues are as follows:

When considering the design of LGBT student support initiatives, what is the nature of the university's political and sociohistorical contexts and how do these influence current levels of LGBT student "outness" and visibility? The student expression of sexual orientation and gender identity at a small, private, politically liberal institution may be very different from that at a large public land-grant institution with a conservative board of regents.

Given political and sociohistorical contexts, how supportive will institutional leadership be of implementing a range of LGBT student support initiatives?

What type of strategic advocacy for LGBT student support initiatives is the best match to secure institutional support?

Are advocacy strategies selected in collaboration with LGBT students in a manner that empowers identity construction and expression?

These questions mirror assumptions of feminist, postmodern, and queer theory perspectives, reflecting ways in which choice of theoretical model may influence decisions about design of campus LGBT student support initiatives.

Beyond the work of student affairs practitioners, the impact of the operating assumptions of an LGBT theoretical framework is also revealed by faculty engaged in teaching and research. Using a feminist perspective in a study of transgender student identity may result in very different conclusions from those drawn from research based on a medical model. For example, a feminist study may reveal ways in which the voices of transgender students are systematically silenced on campus. A medically based study may focus on ways that transitioning from one gender to another may aid transgender students in being more comfortable on campus.

Theoretical operating assumptions may at times be explicit, at others unnamed, but some form of bias is always involved. It is critical that student affairs professionals and scholars are fully conscious of the potential impact that these assumptions bring to their work.

Based on the models presented in this chapter, related student affairs practice and research may express a wide range of assumptions and values. These include such notions as "biology is destiny," "social change occurs only through grassroots empowerment," and "human life unfolds in stages." Regardless of the models of sexual orientation or gender identity selected as the basis for practice and research, it is important that they be thoughtfully examined. Practitioners and scholars have an ethical responsibility to understand what the underlying assumptions of the models are, what each purports to describe, on what populations or premises the models were based, and whose interests are served by different models and their uses.

References

American Psychiatric Association. *Diagnostic and Statistical Manual of Mental Disorders.* (3rd ed.) Washington, D.C.: American Psychiatric Press, 1980.

American Psychiatric Association. *Diagnostic and Statistical Manual of Mental Disorders.* (4th ed., text revision) Washington, D.C.: American Psychiatric Association, 2000.

Becker, D. "Growing Up in Two Closets: Class and Privilege in the Lesbian and Gay Community." In S. Raffo (ed.), *Queerly Classed.* Boston: South End Press, 1997.

Ben-Ari, A. T. "Experiences of 'Not Belonging' in Collectivistic Communities: Narratives of Gays in Kibbutzes." *Journal of Homosexuality,* 2001, 42(2), 101–124.

Besnier, N. "Polynesian Gender Liminality Through Time and Space." In G. Herdt (ed.), *Third Sex, Third Gender: Beyond Sexual Dimorphism in Culture and History.* New York: Zone Books, 1993.

Bilodeau, B. "Beyond the Gender Binary: A Case Study of Transgender College Student Development at a Midwestern University." *Journal of Gay and Lesbian Issues in Education,* 2005, 2(4).

Blumenfeld, W. J., and Raymond, D. *Looking at Gay and Lesbian Life.* (2nd ed.) Boston: Beacon Press, 1993.

Bornstein, K. *Gender Outlaw: On Men, Women and the Rest of Us.* New York: Routledge, 1994.

Boykin, K. *One More River to Cross: Black and Gay in America.* New York: Anchor Books, 1996.

Brown, L. B. "Women and Men, Not-Men and Not-Women, Lesbians and Gays: American Indian Gender Style Alternatives." In L. B. Brown (ed.), *Two Spirit People: American Indian Lesbian Women and Gay Men.* New York: Harrington Park Press, 1997.

Brown, L. S. "Lesbian Identities: Concepts and Issues." In A. R. D'Augelli and C. J. Patterson (eds.), *Lesbian, Gay and Bisexual Identities over the Lifespan.* New York: Oxford University Press, 1995.

Brown, M. L., and Rounsley, C. A. *True Selves: Understanding Transsexualism for Families, Friends, Coworkers, and Helping Professionals.* San Francisco: Jossey-Bass, 1996.

Butler, J. *Gender Trouble: Feminism and the Subversion of Identity.* New York: Routledge, 1990.

Butler, J. *Bodies That Matter: On the Discursive Limits of "Sex."* New York: Routledge, 1993.

Califia, P. *Sex Changes: The Politics of Transgenderism.* San Francisco: Cleis Press, 1997.

Carter, K. A. "Transgenderism and College Students: Issues of Gender Identity and Its Role on Our Campuses." In V. A. Wall, and N. J. Evans (eds.), *Toward Acceptance: Sexual Orientation Issues on Campus.* Washington, D.C.: American College Personnel Association, 2000.

Cass, V. C. "Homosexual Identity Formation: A Theoretical Model." *Journal of Homosexuality,* 1979, 4, 219–235.

Cass, V. C. "Homosexual Identity Formation: Testing a Theoretical Model." *Journal of Sex Research,* 1984, 20, 143–167.

Clare, E. *Exile and Pride: Disability, Queerness, and Liberation.* Boston: South End Press, 1999.

Cooper, K. "Practice with Transgendered Youth and Their Families." In G. P. Mallon (ed.), *Social Services with Transgendered Youth.* Binghamton, N.Y.: Harrington Park Press, 1999.

Creed, B. "Lesbian Bodies: Tribades, Tomboys, and Tarts." In E. Grosz and E. Probyn (eds.), *Sexy Bodies: The Strange Carnalities of Feminism*. New York: Routledge, 1995.

Crow, L., Brown, L. B., and Wright, J. "Gender Selection in Two American Indian Tribes." In L. B. Brown (ed.), *Two Spirit People: American Indian Lesbian Women and Gay Men*. New York: Harrington Park Press, 1997.

D'Augelli, A. R. "Identity Development and Sexual Orientation: Toward a Model of Lesbian, Gay, and Bisexual Development." In E. J. Trickett, R. J. Watts, and D. Birman (eds.), *Human Diversity: Perspectives on People in Context*. San Francisco: Jossey-Bass, 1994.

Denny, D. (ed.). *Current Concepts in Transgender Identity*. New York: Garland, 1998.

Devor, H. *FTM: Female-to-Male Transsexuals in Society*. Bloomington: Indiana University Press, 1997.

Diaz, R. "Latino Gay Men and Psycho-Cultural Barriers to AIDS Prevention." In M. Levine, J. Gagnon, and P. Nardi (eds.), *In Changing Times: Gay Men and Lesbians Encounter HIV/AIDS*. Chicago: University of Chicago Press, 1997.

DuMontier, V. L., II. "Faith, the Bible, and Lesbians, Gay Men, and Bisexuals." In V. A. Wall and N. J. Evans (eds.), *Toward Acceptance: Sexual Orientation Issues on Campus*. Washington, D.C.: American College Personnel Association, 2000.

Elkins, R., and King, D. "Blending Genders—An Introduction." In R. Elkins and D. King (eds.), *Blending Genders: Social Aspects of Cross-Dressing and Sex Changing*. New York: Routledge, 1996.

Erikson, E. *Childhood and Society*. New York: Norton, 1950.

Espin, O. M. "Issues of Identity in the Psychology of Latina Lesbians." In L. S. Garnets and D. C. Kimmel (eds.), *Psychological Perspectives on Lesbian and Gay Male Experiences*. New York: Columbia University Press, 1993.

Evans, N. J., and Broido, E. M. "Coming Out in College Residence Halls: Negotiation, Meaning Making, Challenges, and Supports." *Journal of College Student Development*, 1999, *40*, 658–668.

Fassinger, R. E. "The Hidden Minority: Issues and Challenges in Working with Lesbian Women and Gay Men." *Counseling Psychologist*, 1991, *19*(2), 157–176.

Feinberg, L. *Transgender Warriors: Making History from Joan of Arc to Dennis Rodman*. Boston: Beacon Press, 1996.

Feinberg, L. *Trans Liberation: Beyond Pink or Blue*. Boston: Beacon Press, 1998.

Fox, R. "Bisexual Identities." In A. R. D'Augelli and C. J. Patterson (eds.), *Lesbian, Gay, and Bisexual Identities over the Lifespan: Psychological Perspectives*. New York: Oxford University Press, 1995.

Gonsiorek, J. C. "Gay Male Identities: Concepts and Issues." In A. R. D'Augelli and C. J. Patterson (eds.), *Lesbian, Gay, and Bisexual Identities over the Lifespan: Psychological Perspectives*. New York: Oxford University Press, 1995.

Halberstam, J. *Female Masculinity*. Durham: Duke University Press, 1998.

Harry Benjamin International Gender Dysphoria Association. "The HBIGDA Standards of Care for Gender Identity Disorders, Sixth Version." 2001. http://www.hbigda.org/soc.cfm. Accessed Oct. 20, 2004.

Johnson, M. *Beauty and Power: Transgendering and Cultural Transformation in the Southern Philippines*. New York: Berg, 1997.

Kapack, J. S. "Chinese Male Homosexuality: Sexual Identity Formation and Gay Organizational Development in a Contemporary Chinese Population." Unpublished doctoral dissertation, University of Toronto, 1992.

Klein, F. "The Need to View Sexual Orientation as Multivariable Dynamic Process: A Theoretical Perspective." In D. P. McWhirter, S. A. Sanders, and J. M. Reinisch (eds.), *Homosexuality/Heterosexuality: Concepts of Sexual Orientation*. New York: Oxford University Press, 1990.

Klein, F. *The Bisexual Option*. (2nd ed.) New York: Haworth Press, 1993.

Kovac, A. L. "Africa's Rainbow Nation." *Journal of Southern African Studies*, 2002, *28*(2), 74–82.

Lev, A. I. *Transgender Emergence: Therapeutic Guidelines for Working with Gender-Variant People and Their Families.* New York: Haworth Press, 2004.

Love, P. G. "Cultural Barriers Facing Lesbian, Gay, and Bisexual Students at a Catholic College." *Journal of Higher Education,* 1998, *69,* 298–323.

Mallon, G. P. (ed.). *Social Services with Transgendered Youth.* Binghamton, N.Y.: Harrington Park Press, 1999a.

Mallon, G. P. "Preface: An Ecological Perspective of Social Work Practice with Transgendered Persons." In G. P. Mallon (ed.), *Social Services with Transgendered Youth.* Binghamton, N.Y.: Harrington Park Press, 1999b.

Manalansan, M. "(Re)Locating the Gay Filipino: Resistance, Postcolonialism, and Identity." *Journal of Homosexuality,* 1993, *26(2/3),* 53–73.

Marcia, J. E. "Identity in Adolescence." In J. Adelson (ed.), *Handbook of Adolescent Psychiatry.* New York: Wiley, 1980.

McLelland, M. *Male Homosexuality in Modern Japan: Cultural Myths and Social Realities.* Richmond, Va.: Corson Press, 2000.

O'Keefe, T., and Fox, K. *Trans-x-u-all: The Naked Difference.* London: Extraordinary People Press, 1997.

Raffo, S. "Introduction." In S. Raffo (ed.), *Queerly Classed.* Boston: South End Press, 1997.

Renn, K. A., and Bilodeau, B. "Queer Student Leaders: A Case Study of Identity Development and Lesbian, Gay, Bisexual, and Transgender Student Involvement at a Midwestern Research University." *Journal of Gay and Lesbian Issues in Education,* 2005, 3(1).

Rhoads, R. A. *Coming Out in College: The Struggle for a Queer Identity.* Westport, Conn.: Bergin and Garvey, 1994.

Ryan, C., and Futterman, D. *Lesbian and Gay Youth: Care and Counseling.* New York: Columbia University Press, 1998.

Savin-Williams, R. C. "Theoretical Perspectives Accounting for Adolescent Homosexuality." *Journal of Adolescent Health,* 1988, *9(6),* 95–104.

Savin-Williams, R. C. "Gay and Lesbian Adolescents." *Marriage and Family Review,* 1990, *14,* 197–216.

Sears, J. T. "The Impact of Gender and Race on Growing up Lesbian and Gay in the South." *National Women's Studies Association Journal,* 1989, *1,* 422–457.

Troiden, R. R. "Becoming Homosexual: A Model of Gay Identity Acquisition." *Psychiatry,* 1979, *42,* 362–373.

Troiden, R. R. "Homosexual Identity Development." *Journal of Adolescent Health Care,* 1988, *9,* 105–113.

Vanderbosh, J. "Notes from the Working Class." In S. Raffo (ed.), *Queerly Classed.* Boston: South End Press, 1997.

Wilchins, R. A. *Read My Lips: Sexual Subversion and the End of Gender.* New York: Firebrand Books, 1997.

Wilchins, R. A. "Queerer Bodies." In J. Nestle, C. Howell, and R. A. Wilchins (eds.), *Genderqueer: Voices from Beyond the Sexual Binary.* Los Angeles: Alyson, 2002.

Wilson, A. "How We Find Ourselves: Identity Development in Two-Spirit People." *Harvard Educational Review,* 1996, *66(2),* 303–317.

BRENT L. BILODEAU *is director of the Office of LGBT Concerns and a doctoral candidate in higher, adult, and lifelong education at Michigan State University.*

KRISTEN A. RENN *is assistant professor of higher, adult, and lifelong education at Michigan State University.*

The intersection of race, faith, and sexual orientation is a complicated place. This chapter examines students with these multiple identities and uses theory and personal accounts to illustrate the challenges of navigating community on campus.

Multiple Identities: Creating Community on Campus for LGBT Students

Kerry John Poynter, Jamie Washington

The popularity of public figures such as Ellen Degeneres and Rosie O'Donnell, and of television programs such as *Will and Grace, Queer Eye for the Straight Guy,* and *Queer as Folk,* suggest that mainstream audiences are tolerating and, perhaps, accepting lesbian, gay, bisexual, and transgender (LGBT) people. More often than not, however, these entertainers and television shows reflect only one LGBT community, one whose members are white and not religious. This perception of the LGBT community is common on college and university campuses, too. As one African American student commented:

> I had been a member of BSA (Black Student Association) my freshman year, but was discouraged when I consistently encountered homophobic attitudes in the organization. My friends and I often laughed at our slogan for it, 'It's either Gay or BSA!' We also couldn't help but notice the undercurrent of racism within the gay community. It was passive and subtle, but clear. Our white LGBT peers felt as though the LGBT student organization was not meeting their needs because programming and social events were too ethnic or "did not reflect who they were or their interests" [Mills, 2005, n.p.].

A gay seminary student noted similar experiences:

I feel caught in the middle. It's a guarded situation. At the divinity school I face a lot of stereotypes that you would assume a Christian organization would have about homosexuality. Likewise, as a Christian you face stereotypes that homosexuals have for Christians. The main thing for me is that there is no welcoming community for people like me. Community is something that you have to create for yourself. The small group of gay Christians I brought together is a community that we built, but my experience in the [LGBT] Center is that LGBT students look at us from a distance. It is the same way that the divinity students look at the gay divinity students. "I'm not part of them." They see the differences and not the commonalities [P. Shoe, personal communication, January 18, 2005].

As these quotations illustrate, developing or finding community can be a difficult task when sexual orientation, race, and faith collide. As student affairs professionals, we have a duty to understand the students and student populations with whom we work. We should expect that LGBT students on our campuses comprise much diversity. "Gay" does not always imply white or atheist. To this end we discuss the intersection of race, faith, and sexual orientation and share some of the complexities of finding and creating community.

The Intersections of Identity Development Theory

It may be best to view the development of students with multiple identities not as a linear series of stages, but as complex processes of simultaneous tasks and challenges. The multiple identities of an LGBT person interact with and affect one another. The development of one identity— such as race—can cause regression or progress in another, such as sexual orientation. A questioning of previous beliefs caused by the development of one identity can create dissonance to be resolved only by greater understanding of how these multiple identities can benefit one another. This resolution can occur satisfactorily in conditions that provide contact with other multiple-identity LGBT people and groups within the context of affirming environments.

Identity Development Theory

Theories of identity development rarely address overlapping and multiple identities and how they intersect. Such monocultural or single-focused theories have an inherent limitation in that they do not consider how other minority or cultural identities affect developmental processes. We recognize this limitation (see Chapter Three for a more complete examination) and use the three theories explained here, in brief, as a framework to begin to create a better understanding of the intersection of multiple identities.

LGB Identity Development. Fassinger (Fassinger and Miller, 1997; McCarn and Fassinger, 1996) explains LGB sexual identity development as along two parallel branches: the individual and the group. The group branch is defined by how an individual "identifies with or actively participates in gay or lesbian culture(s)" (Fassinger and Miller, 1996, p. 55). How an LGB student identifies or views the LGBT campus community influences this group branch. Further development along this group identity will be partly dependent on integrating other identities, such as faith.

Faith Development. "Faith is how people become aware of self, others, and the transcendent. It is how people make meaning out of, and commitment based upon what they have become, learned, or discovered" (DuMontier, 2000, p. 323). Organized religion has not been welcoming of—and in some cases has been hostile to—LGBT people. While there has been much progress on this front, the importance of this hostile environment cannot be underestimated or considered lightly. This hostility can directly influence the faith development of an LGBT student. Fowler explains faith development in six stages. Stage four, "individual-reflective faith," occurs when an individual "begins to define and take responsibility for a world view that is internally driven" (as quoted in DuMontier, 2000, p. 325). Thus, developing an LGBT identity might create a need to find a faith community or an LGBT community that is affirming and supportive of a person's faith and sexual or gender identity. "This requires a genuine openness to others and a willingness to enter into dialogue . . . even at the risk of changing a person's own way of making meaning and relating to the world" (Rutledge, 1989, p. 21).

Racial Identity Development. Individuals of a racial minority might not identify with an LGBT community seen largely as white and thus will not readily accept a sexual identity as LGBT. Cross's five-stage model of racial identity development (1971) describes processes of encounter, immersion, and internalization. How does being non-heterosexual affect these particular identity stages for a person of color? Perhaps they will "attempt to shift the conflict from a monocultural perspective (i.e. either Latino or LGBT) to a multicultural dimension (Latino and LGBT) in which their lives can be viewed as containing multiple identities" (Chan, 1995, p. 93).

A Just Community

Among Boyer's six principles of campus community is the assertion that "a college or university is a just community, a place where the sacredness of each person is honored and where diversity is aggressively pursued" (1990, p. 25). Although Boyer emphasized diversity of race and sex in his original description of a just community, surely a reevaluation of this work today could not ignore LGBT students. Recognition of people with multiple identities or multiple minority identities must be constructed on campus as well as learning across those differences. Boyer also explains, in his description of an open community, that "the quality of a college . . . must be measured by the quality of communication on campus" that includes "clarity of expression" and "civility" (p. 17). The students with whom we work should be listening to, and learning from, one another as well as speaking across homogenous and monocultural lines.

Making Connections

Student affairs administrators play a key role in creating connections between and among oppressed and privileged groups on campus. Administrators need to manage a difficult balance between the desires and needs of monocultural or homogenous groups and the need for cross-cultural communication and learning. The challenge remains that students often are not found conversing across such delineations of privilege and oppression and segregate themselves in homogeneous communities of comfort.

Organizations of LGBT students, as well as those of other minority groups, have been accused of self-segregation. Yet many other student organizations are composed of homogeneous interests. Athletes, Bible-study groups, marching-band members, and sociology students are just a few examples of students who congregate and communicate on the basis of common interests and identities. In the same way, LGBT and race-based groups form for mutual support as well as to create a basis for connection to the broader campus community. Widespread intolerance, lack of acceptance, and the failure of the campus community to create hospitable campus climates also contribute to the formation of minority student organizations (Tatum, 1999).

The need and inclination to be with those similar to oneself create conflicts for students with multiple identities. Multiple-identity LGBT people have to contend with racism and religious intolerance from within the LGBT community and from homophobia within the various heterosexual minority and religious communities. Rejection in the form of racism and homophobia creates an almost insurmountable hurdle to finding community. Yet without spaces for open and authentic conversations across multiple minority identities, true community cannot be achieved.

One student commented on this dilemma: "My job is doubly hard. I have to help educate not only the straight community about gay issues but I also have to educate the black community, and that's next to impossible. Homophobia is really strong with the black community" (Rhoads, 1994, p. 135).

A Christian LGBT student shared his experience in his own faith community on campus: "When we talk about LGBT issues and faith the response is, 'It's already been talked about.' The problem is that incoming students are not part of that situation and they have to face those issues over and over again. The divinity school talked about gay people in response to the covenant code before I arrived on campus and now they think they discussed homosexuality" (P. Shoe, personal communication, January 18, 2005).

An African American student described his attempt to connect with a gay student group on campus:

> When I first came here I tried to reach out to (the student group) LGBSA, and when I went to one of the meetings it took me a half-hour just to work up the courage to walk into the room. When I got there I saw that there was nobody else who was black except maybe for one other person. After the meeting not a single person walked up to me and introduced themselves. No one said anything to me. Then this guy on my floor who claimed to be straight was doing a paper for a class on gays and so he went to an LGBSA meeting. He is tall, has good features, and is attractive and white. He went to a meeting and after it was over he said two or three people came up to him and introduced themselves and were very friendly to him. He talked about his paper on our hall one time, and I remember thinking to myself, 'This can't be the same meeting I went to.' It really woke me up to the white gay community and its racism" [Rhoads, 1994, p. 136].

All of these examples illustrate challenges for multiple-identity minority students. Student affairs professionals must ask themselves how they can support these students and create communities that are safe for learning and exploration. To work effectively with these differences we must understand how students make meaning of these multiple identities.

Navigating Multiple-Identity Conflict

How do multiple-identity LGBT people shift from being either a person of color or a person who is religious to a person who integrates these identities? Does integration of identities occur? Possible outcomes include identifying with multiple groups and integrating these identities (such as viewing oneself as both African American and lesbian), identifying with one group exclusively to the detriment of others (for example, a woman portrays herself as Native American culturally and spiritually yet ignores a public LGBT identity due to fear of reprisal in a dominant Christian environment), or identifying with one group at a given time (for example, a Latino male identifies himself as gay in a predominantly white LGBT community yet does not do so among Latino friends and family) (Reynolds and Pope, 1991).

Language is one of the major challenges in understanding and engaging multiple identities. For African Americans, for example, the terms *lesbian, gay, bisexual,* and *transgender* are often associated with white culture (Boykin, 1996). As a result, many people of color distance themselves from these terms and have crafted others, as described by Boykin (2005):

- *Same-gender loving.* Often used by people of color who are comfortable with their same-sex attraction but do not connect with the social and political connotations that come with the terms *lesbian, gay, bisexual,* and *transgender*

- *Men who have sex with men.* A term created by the Centers for Disease Control in 1987 to describe men who do not use the labels *gay* or *bisexual* but who participate in same-sex sexual behaviors
- *DL,* or *Down Low.* A new term popular in the black and Latino communities referring to men who do not identify themselves as gay but who have sex with men as well as with female partners.

Each of these terms carries social and political implications that cannot be addressed in this short piece. It is important to note, however, that the common denominator is same-sex attraction or connection. Understanding the complexities that culture, community, and religion bring to sexual minorities is important if we are to create environments where these individuals can grow.

Implications for Student Affairs Practice

As we enter these uncharted waters, the professional literature in student affairs provides little information to identify best practices. However, groups such as the National Consortium of Directors of LGBT Resources in Higher Education, the National Gay and Lesbian Task Force (NGLTF), and the American College Personnel Association (ACPA) Standing Committee for LGBT Awareness are initiating ongoing discussions within their respective organizations and collaboratively with one another to assist in developing supportive and responsive communities for students with multiple minority identities.

Campus staff must be fully engaged in creating a cross-cultural community that is just, civil, and open. Avenues of expression need to be created that provide spaces, programs, classroom discussions, and living-learning communities about and for multiple-minority students. The following five suggestions are intended to foster discussion and thought about the issues raised in this chapter:

- Allow students to "name" themselves and their identities. Don't ask them to choose one identity over the other.
- Engage all students in discussions of their race, religion, and other identities.
- Work with campus religious leaders and the multicultural or ethnic offices and leaders to engage and address issues of sexual orientation and gender identity.
- Seek opportunities to bring expert speakers to campus, and seek campus role models to speak to the complexities of multiple identities that include being a sexual minority.

References

Boyer, E. L. *Campus Life: In Search of Community*. Princeton, N.J.: Carnegie Foundation for the Advancement of Teaching, 1990.

Boykin, K. *One More River to Cross: Black and Gay in America*. New York: Anchor Books, 1996.

Boykin, K. *Beyond the Down Low: Sex, Lies, and Denial in Black America*. New York: Carrol and Graf, 2005.

Chan, C. S. "Issues of Sexual Identity in an Ethnic Minority: The Case of Chinese American Lesbians, Gay Men, and Bisexual People." In A. R. D'Augelli and C. J. Patterson (eds.), *Lesbian, Gay and Bisexual Identities over the Lifespan: Psychological Perspectives*. New York: Oxford University Press, 1995.

Cross, W. E. "The Negro-to-Black Conversion Experience: Toward a Psychology of Black Liberation." *Black World*, 1971, *20*, 13–27.

DuMontier, V. L. "Faith, the Bible, and Lesbians, Gay Men, and Bisexuals." In V. A. Wall and N. J. Evans (eds.), *Toward Acceptance: Sexual Orientation Issues on Campus*. Alexandria, Va: American College Personnel Association, 2000.

Fassinger, R. E., and Miller, B. A. "Validation of an Inclusive Model of Homosexual Identity Formation in a Sample of Gay Men." *Journal of Homosexuality,* 1997, *32*, 53–78.

McCarn, S. R., and Fassinger, R. E. "Revisioning Sexual Minority Identity Formation: A New Model of Lesbian Identity and Its Implications for Counseling and Research." *Counseling Psychologist*, 1996, *24*(3), 508–534.

Mills, C. "Free . . . Almost." 2004. http://www.keithboykin.com/arch/001278.html. Accessed Jan. 18, 2005.

Reynolds, A. L., and Pope, R. L. "The Complexities of Diversity: Exploring Multiple Oppressions." *Journal of Counseling and Development*, 1991, *70*, 174–180.

Rhoads, R. A. *Coming Out in College: The Struggle for a Queer Identity*. Westport, Conn.: Bergin and Garvey, 1994.

Rutledge, M. "Faith: Bridging Theory and Practice." In J. Butler (ed.), *Religion on Campus*. New Directions for Student Services, no. 46. San Francisco: Jossey-Bass, 1989.

Tatum, B. D. *Why Are All the Black Kids Sitting Together in the Cafeteria?* New York: Basic Books, 1999.

KERRY JOHN POYNTER is program director for the LGBT Center at Duke University.

JAMIE WASHINGTON was assistant vice president for student affairs at the University of Maryland Baltimore County and is a founding faculty member of the Social Justice Training Institute.

5

Colleges and universities are beginning to consider the needs of transgender students, but few understand how to offer support to this segment of the campus community. This chapter address issues and provides suggestions for student affairs professionals.

Transgender Issues on College Campuses

Brett Beemyn, Billy Curtis, Masen Davis, Nancy Jean Tubbs

Anecdotal evidence suggests that students are coming out as transgender on campuses across the country. The term *transgender* encompasses a wide range of identities, appearances, and behaviors that blur or cross gender lines. Within this transgender umbrella are transsexuals, who live some or all of the time in a sex different from their biological sex; cross-dressers (formerly called transvestites), who wear clothes typically associated with the "opposite" gender; drag kings and drag queens, who cross-dress within a performance context; and genderqueers, who identify outside of binary gender or sex systems (Lombardi and Davis, forthcoming).

This chapter discusses the experiences of transgender students and how student affairs professionals may effectively address these students' needs in areas of campus life where transgender students have unique concerns: programming, housing, bathrooms and locker rooms, counseling and health care, and records and documents. Although a growing number of colleges and universities are beginning to consider the needs of transgender students, most institutions still offer little or no support to this segment of the campus community (Transgender Law and Policy Institute, 2005). If student affairs professionals are committed to working with all students and helping foster their personal development and academic success, then they cannot ignore transgender students. As this chapter demonstrates, transgender students regularly encounter institutional discrimination in higher education, which makes it particularly important that student affairs professionals understand their experiences and the obstacles they confront at most colleges and universities.

NEW DIRECTIONS FOR STUDENT SERVICES, no. 111, Fall 2005 © Wiley Periodicals, Inc.

Who Are Transgender Students?

Transgender students may be of any age, ethnicity, race, class, or sexual orientation. Some enter higher education open about being transgender, while others come out during college or graduate school. Still others may never use the term *transgender*, but will strongly identify themselves as male, female, transsexual, or another (or no) gender. Some students may choose to transition; that is, to live as a gender different from the one assigned to them at birth. Transitioning is a complex, individual process that often includes changing one's name, appearance, and body (Lombardi and Davis, forthcoming).

Identity development is a dynamic process for many transgender college students (Bilodeau, 2005). Consider the following composite portraits that represent but a fraction of the diverse identities of and challenges faced by transgender students. Sky, for example, entered college as a lesbian. During her sophomore year, she realized she felt like neither a woman nor a man and began identifying as genderqueer. Over time, Sky identified as an effeminate gay man, but found it difficult to find male partners as a gender-different student. During Sky's senior year, he initiated hormone treatment and lived as a man.

Many transgender students experience isolation and rejection from family and friends (Pusch, 2005). Curt, an eighteen-year-old heterosexual male, had been placed into foster care after being rejected by his family when he came out as a female-to-male transsexual two years earlier. Now in his first year of college, Curt is legally changing his name and gender. He is frustrated that professors keep calling him by his female name even though he presents as male and has asked to be called Curt. He feels isolated and is considering leaving school.

Transgender students confront a number of challenges within campus environments, including a lack of access to health care and difficulties with sex-segregated facilities (Beemyn, 2003; Nakamura, 1998). Maria, a Latina student, was assigned male at birth. Although Maria would prefer that no one know that she is a transsexual woman, she must negotiate with student health to ensure access to hormones and other services. Maria works extra hours so she can afford genital surgery some day.

Other students live genderqueer lives by refusing to limit themselves to any single gender. Ron, a nineteen-year-old African American male, proudly wears a dress around campus, weathering chronic harassment from other students. Chris, a graduate student, wants to be gender-free and prefers gender-neutral pronouns.

Transgender students offer unique contributions to the campus community. With the assistance of student service professionals who can help them navigate campus resources and sex-segregated facilities, transgender students can fully realize their potential.

Addressing Specific Transgender Concerns

Primary issue areas regarding the concerns of transgender students are described here.

Programming. College events and activities play a significant role in a student's sense of belonging and connection with the greater campus community. The quality and quantity of a student's involvement on campus also has a positive effect on the student's learning and development (Astin, 1984). Institutions should thus develop programs that are welcoming to transgender students, including programs that focus specifically on transgender issues. A campus with a variety of events and activities that are inclusive of transgender experiences and needs can also provide nontrans-gender students with a more valuable college experience.

Educational Programs. In order for transgender students to feel welcomed and included in campus life and activities, programming must reflect their experiences and allow for their full participation. Similar to other underrepresented communities on campus, transgender students may feel invisible or marginalized if little or no effort is made to acknowledge their presence, much less meet their needs. Yet most campuses offer few opportunities for students to learn about transgender issues and experiences (Beemyn, 2003; Sausa, 2002).

Creating and widely advertising transgender-focused educational programs can increase campus awareness of the unique challenges faced by transgender students. Colleges and universities can also develop a transgender ally program or speakers bureau, create a transgender FAQ bulletin board packet for residence halls, invite leading transgender speakers to campus, schedule a separate awareness week for transgender issues, include transgender-related information throughout the institution's Web site, and offer regular training sessions for staff and students on transgender issues.

Support Services. Support for transgender students is typically combined with support for lesbian, gay, and bisexual (LGB) students. But many LGB student organizations and academic programs, even ones that include or have added "transgender" to their names in recent years, rarely address gender identity issues and often provide limited support to transgender students, especially to transgender students who self-identify as heterosexual (Beemyn, 2003). As a result, transgender students are forming their own groups at some colleges and universities, particularly where there are a large number of openly transgender students and a more supportive campus climate. In the absence of a transgender student organization, a campus LGBT office or counseling center can work with students to create a transgender support group (Beemyn, 2003; Lees, 1998).

Inclusive Policies. Campus nondiscrimination policies include the categories of "sex" and sometimes "sexual orientation," but neither category necessarily covers transgender people, who face discrimination based on their gender identity and expression rather than their biological gender or sexual identity (Beemyn, 2003). To protect the rights of transgender people, more than twenty colleges and college systems have added protection of "gender identity or expression" to their nondiscrimination policies. A number of institutions are also changing policies and practices that exclude or marginalize transgender students by conceptualizing gender as male and female, such as college forms that allow students to identify only as male or female (Transgender Law and Policy Institute, 2005). (See also Chapter One of this volume.)

Campus Housing. Housing policies and practices that assume that students are male or female fail to serve transgender students, especially those who are in the process of transitioning from one gender to another or who do not identify as either dominant gender. If college administrators are to continue to meet the changing needs of students, they must develop procedures that recognize diverse gender identities and expressions. This professional obligation is also a legal requirement at institutions where state or municipal laws or college policies ban discrimination against people because of their gender identity or expression.

Given the diversity of individual student needs and the immense diversity of housing facilities and programs, the housing needs of transgender students must be addressed on a case-by-case basis. However, a formal written policy can guide institutional practice and provide a foundation for ensuring the fair, safe, and legal treatment of transgender students.

Several colleges and universities have adopted such housing policies. The University of Minnesota, Twin Cities, developed a policy that respects the gender identity a student establishes with the university and strives to provide accommodations when possible (Transgender Law and Policy Institute, 2005). The Ohio State University created a similar policy, which also states that no student "whom they know to be transgendered [will] have to find a comfortable, welcoming housing assignment on their own" (Ohio State University, 2005). The policy of the University of California, Riverside, emphasizes the principle of "reasonable accommodations" when the University is notified in a timely manner (University of California, Riverside, 2005).

In order to identify and assist transgender students, some colleges and universities are changing the sex designation on their housing intake forms (Transgender Law and Policy Institute, 2005). Asking if someone is male or female not only fails to recognize the full complexity of gender identity, but also provides insufficient information for roommate assignments. More appropriate alternatives to binary boxes are simple fill-in-the-blank options, "Your gender is: _____," or the multiple choices of "Male," "Female," "Self-Identify: _____." Housing forms also often ask students to indicate any special needs. Some campuses include "transgender" or "gender different" among these concerns (Transgender Law and Policy Institute, 2005).

Regardless of how transgender students notify the institution of their gender identities, residence-life staff should follow up with students who want to live on campus to understand their specific needs better. In such instances, the personal information shared by the students should be kept confidential, and only information required to establish the need for a particular accommodation should be requested. Some transgender students prefer not to reveal the status of their physical body, which may not be congruent with their gender identity or expression. Colleges and universities should thus allow students to demonstrate the need for a particular housing option by providing a letter from a medical professional.

Residence-life staff who demonstrate their sensitivity to and understanding of transgender experiences create a welcoming environment for students to explore their housing needs and options more honestly and effectively. However, many colleges and universities have yet to identify the campus housing options that would provide the safest and most comfortable living arrangements for transgender students.

Implementing policies supportive of trans students requires student affairs staff to assess different housing options in relation to transgender student needs. Many campus residence halls were built at a time when hallways, floors, or buildings were divided by gender and offered only communal men's and women's restrooms and shower rooms. By inventorying the kinds of facilities available and how students are housed in these facilities, residence-life staff can successfully address the needs of transgender students on a case-by-case basis (Curtis and Tubbs, 2004).

When assessing housing facilities, the first consideration is whether rooms are co-ed or same-sex by suite, hallway, floor, or building. A transgender student's ability to "pass" may be more difficult in a same-sex living environment, where residents are expected to conform to a particular set of gender expressions.

Residence-life staff should document the existence and location of rooms that have their own bathrooms and showers. As discussed later in this chapter, many transgender students prefer private restrooms and shower facilities for safety reasons. In residence halls that do not have a bathroom in each room, residence-life staff should note whether the buildings have any gender-neutral restrooms and whether any of the shower facilities have lockable stalls, rather than just shower curtains. They should also examine cost differences between residence halls to determine whether transgender students are forced to incur a greater financial burden in order to live in a safer environment.

Another important consideration is which buildings or floors include theme housing, and whether transgender students would likely gain acceptance and feel a part of these communities. Even an LGBT and Allies theme hall may not be a comfortable environment for transgender students if they identify as heterosexual or are not open about their gender identity.

A campus housing assessment should also examine the demographics of the residents of each building. Returning students who have already lived on campus may be more accepting of gender difference, and thus a largely upper-class-student residence hall might be a safer location for transgender students.

Recognizing that existing facilities are often unable to meet the needs of students with diverse gender identities, some colleges and universities are beginning to offer a gender-neutral housing option, either to all students or just to upper-class students. In gender-neutral housing, room assignments are made without regard to the individuals' biological gender, so residents may request a roommate of any gender. Among the institutions that provide this opportunity are Sarah Lawrence College, the University of California, Riverside, the University of Pennsylvania, the University of Southern Maine, and Wesleyan University (Curtis and Tubbs, 2004; Transgender Law and Policy Institute, 2005).

Because transgender students have unique concerns that are often poorly understood by housing staff, regular training workshops for professionals and paraprofessionals in residence life are essential for meeting the needs of transgender students. In addition to providing basic information about transgender people, these sessions should address how to make room assignments for transgender students, how to assist a student who comes out as transgender during the academic year, how to create trans-inclusive hall programs, and how to create a safe, confidential space so that transgender students feel comfortable approaching staff with questions and concerns.

To inform current and prospective students about how the campus addresses the housing needs of transgender people, colleges and universities should include such information, along with the contact information of a housing staff person who can respond to transgender-related questions and concerns, on residence-life Web sites and brochures and in any material targeted to LGBT communities. Housing staff should also seek to reach prospective students through sharing the information with student affairs colleagues, particularly the staffs in admissions, orientation, and student activities. Returning students might be reached through outreach to campus groups or offices that provide support to LGBT students.

Student affairs professionals should recognize transgender students' needs, just as they would try to understand and address the concerns of members of other underrepresented communities. By acknowledging and accommodating the specific housing needs of transgender students and fostering a residential environment where all forms of diversity are celebrated and appreciated, residence-life staff can help transgender students benefit both academically and socially from living on campus.

Bathrooms and Locker Rooms. Whether through cross-dressing, transitioning from one gender to another, or blending traditionally female and male elements, transgender students violate society's expectation that someone is either female or male, which makes them vulnerable to harassment and violence. Some of the most dangerous places on many campuses for transgender students are restrooms and locker rooms designated for "women" and "men." Anecdotal and research evidence suggest that transgender people often face verbal and physical assault and risk being questioned or even arrested by the police when they use gender-specific facilities (Coalition for Queer Action, 2001; San Francisco Human Rights Commission, 2001).

Given these dangers, it is not surprising that using bathrooms and locker rooms presents a major source of anxiety for many transgender students. Some travel far out of their way to use restrooms that are safer and more private, or avoid using campus bathrooms altogether, to the detriment of their comfort and health (Coalition for Queer Action, 2001). It is easier for transgender people to avoid using locker rooms, where having to undress and shower in front of others may "out" them as transgender. But transgender students are thus prevented from being able to participate in athletic programs and physical education courses and from having complete access to campus recreational facilities.

To aid transgender people in being able to use bathrooms without fear or concern, students, staff, and faculty at some colleges are advocating for the creation of gender-neutral restrooms (single-stall, lockable, unisex restrooms) in existing and newly constructed buildings. For example, the student association at San Diego State University passed a resolution in 2003 calling for the implementation of safe restrooms across campus for transgender students. As a first step, the group approved funds to change door signs and install door locks to convert a set of women's and men's bathrooms in the student union into gender-neutral facilities. The locations of all gender-neutral restrooms are also listed in the university's general catalog. At the University of Chicago and at Beloit College (Wisconsin), students successfully lobbied their institutions to create gender-neutral bathrooms in the most frequented campus buildings (Transgender Law and Policy Institute, 2005).

To make locker rooms safe for transgender students, colleges and universities can create individual showers with curtains or private changing rooms. Although these changes require more extensive renovations than converting men's and women's restrooms into gender-neutral bathrooms, institutions should have facilities that are accessible to all members of the campus community. Moreover, private changing rooms benefit not only transgender people, but also families with children (such as mothers bringing sons or fathers bringing daughters to a facility) and people with disabilities who require the assistance of an attendant of a different gender.

Counseling and Health Care. As transgender students become increasingly visible on college campuses, counseling and health care services are struggling to address the unique needs of this population (Beemyn, 2003; Carter, 2000). For example, a 2002 survey of University of Michigan student affairs professionals, including counselors and health care providers, found that more than half of the respondents reported challenges in addressing the concerns of transgender students (Gender Identity Working Group, 2003). A related survey of more than four hundred University of Michigan students (Matney, 2003) found that transgender students there face multiple barriers, including perceptions that campus health care and counseling professionals are unable to provide support to transgender students or adequately address their needs.

Other colleges and universities likewise lack supportive health care services for transgender students. In a national qualitative study of seventy-five transgender undergraduate and graduate students, McKinney (2005) found that only four of the respondents indicated positive interactions with campus counselors. Many of the graduate students in the study also reported that campus health center staff failed to provide adequate services for transgender students.

Counseling. Culturally appropriate counseling can provide a safe, nonjudgmental place for students to explore their developing identities and address college-related challenges (Gould, 2004). While sharing many of the same developmental concerns as their peers, transgender students may also face culturally specific issues related to their gender-identity development, including coming out to themselves and to family and friends, negotiating gendered environments (such as residence halls and restrooms), deciding whether or not to transition physically to the "opposite" sex, negotiating intimate relationships outside of traditional male and female identities, accessing health care services supportive of transgender people, adjusting to a new social identity, and surviving discrimination and harassment (Ettner and Brown, 1999; Gould, 2004; Israel and Tarver, 1997). Counselors working with students who are seeking to transition should refer to the Standards of Care developed by the Harry Benjamin International Gender Dysphoria Association (2001) for recommended treatment guidelines.

The scant research that has been published on transgender students finds that they are subject to higher rates of marginalization, discrimination, and harassment than nontransgender students (Rankin, 2003). The social and economic stresses that many transgender students experience as a result of family rejection, harassment, violence, and isolation can, in turn, lead to adjustment disorders, depression, posttraumatic stress, anxiety, depression, substance abuse, suicide ideation, and self-harm (Dean, 2000). These mental health issues may affect the academic success of transgender students, making access to supportive counseling even more important for this population. Although counseling may be encouraged for transgender people, especially for those who plan to undergo gender reassignment processes, being transgender should not be considered a mental illness (Dean, 2000). A diagnosis of a gender-related mental disorder should be limited to individuals with evidence of distress or impairment of functioning beyond that caused by social stigma or prejudice (American Psychiatric Association, 1994).

Health Care. All students need and deserve culturally competent primary health care to maintain healthy, productive lives. Although research on campus-based health services for transgender people is sparse, studies of general health care access for this population find that professionals typically lack accurate information about transgender people, severely limiting their ability to provide quality care (Dean, 2000). For example, a survey of transgender men in Los Angeles (FTM Alliance of Los Angeles, 2004) found that slightly more than half of the respondents had been denied medical services because of their transgender status. When they did receive care, more than two-thirds were dissatisfied with the provider's knowledge of transgender issues. A Washington, D.C., transgender needs assessment (Xavier, 2000) reported that nearly one-third of the 263 transgender people surveyed believed that the transphobia of health care providers and a fear that caregivers would disclose their transgender status were barriers to medical care. In one of the few college-based studies, McKinney (2005) found that transgender graduate students were more concerned than their undergraduate peers about health issues. The graduate student participants did not feel that campus health care systems met their needs—they often had to educate the providers about transgender health issues—and their limited health insurance coverage made it difficult for them to seek off-campus health care.

In order to provide more competent and supportive health care, campus health center staff should educate themselves on transgender health issues and the specific needs of transgender people. For example, health care providers should recognize that the external appearance of a transgender student may differ significantly from the person's internal anatomy. Thus a transsexual man may need a pap smear if he has not had a hysterectomy, and a transsexual woman may need a prostate exam (Feldman and Bockting, 2003). In addition to informed and sensitive primary health care, transgender students need access to gender-specific services, including safe, affordable hormones and gender-related surgeries. If campus health insurance plans exclude transition-related services, student health personnel should advocate for expanded coverage and help students find alternate, off-campus care. The absence of appropriate health care may have a negative affect on the retention, academic success, and physical and mental well-being of transgender students (DeBerard, Spielmans, and Julka, 2004; Lombardi and Davis, forthcoming).

Campuses across the country are beginning to improve the quality of health services for transgender students (McKinney, 2005). For example, the University of Michigan and the University of Minnesota have health care and counseling programs specific to transgender people, and the University of California, Berkeley, has developed a Transgender Student Health Web site to create a welcoming climate and increase health access for transgender students (University of California, Berkeley, Health Services, 2004; University of Michigan Health System Comprehensive Gender Services Program, 2004; University of Minnesota Transgender Health Services, 2004). Some colleges and universities are also implementing mandatory transgender education training sessions for health center staff, revising intake forms to be inclusive of transgender students and developing policies and procedures to help ensure that transgender students receive appropriate and supportive health services (Transgender Law and Policy Institute, 2005).

Institutions that are unable to meet the health care needs of transgender students should develop a resource guide and referral system for off-campus, transgender-friendly counselors and health providers. In the absence of local resources, students may be referred to relevant national organizations, publications, and Web sites, such as Trans-Health (http://www.trans-health.com) and TransGenderCare (http://www.transgendercare.com).

College Records and Documents. Transsexual students who decide to transition from one gender to another typically seek to change their gender and often their names on official records and documents. Students who self-identify as genderqueer may also change their given names to match their gender identity. The process for making these changes varies from state to state and institution to institution. At some colleges and universities, the process is difficult or no means exist to make such changes.

Being able to alter their records and documents, though, is personally and legally important for many transgender students. Not only does having the appropriate name and gender reflect and validate their identities, but it may also prevent transgender students from being placed into uncomfortable and dangerous situations where they would have to explain why they use a name different from their birth name and why their appearance does not match a photo or gender designation on an identification card. Moreover, updated records and documents ensure that transgender students will not be forced to disclose their gender identities and thus be subject to discrimination when they apply for jobs, seek admission to graduate and professional schools, or at any other time when they must show a college document.

Colleges can address this issue by establishing a simple procedure for transgender students to change the name or gender designation on all of their campus records, including ID cards, listings in electronic and print directories, and files in admissions, financial aid, the registrar's office, and the health center. For example, at Ohio State University, transgender students who legally change their names can complete a form with the registrar to change the name as well as the gender designation on their main college record. At the University of Maryland, transgender students can change the name and gender listed on their records by obtaining a letter of support from a mental health professional. Through these processes, students at both institutions effectively change the information on all of their campus records. No one outside of the registrar's offices knows that students' records have been changed. At the University of Vermont, transgender students who are not in a position to change their names legally can still request an ID card with a name other than their birth name (Transgender Law and Policy Institute, 2005).

An institution should never insist that individuals have genital surgeries before changing their records. More and more transsexual students are identifying and living as a gender different from their birth gender without pursuing or completing gender reassignment, and even people who desire surgeries often cannot afford the procedures or are limited by pre-existing medical conditions. Moreover, some transmen feel that the results of genitoplasty (genital reconstruction) are less than adequate. Given these factors, it is inappropriate and unethical for institutions to pressure students to have surgery before aligning their records with their identities.

References

American Psychiatric Association. *Diagnostic and Statistical Manual of Mental Disorders.* (4th ed.) Washington, D.C.: American Psychiatric Association, 1994.

Astin, A. W. "Student Involvement: A Developmental Theory for Higher Education." *Journal of College Student Personnel,* 1984, *25,* 297–308.

Beemyn, B. "Serving the Needs of Transgender College Students." *Journal of Gay and Lesbian Issues in Education,* 2003, *1*(1), 33–50.

Bilodeau, B. "Beyond the Gender Binary: New Perspectives on Transgender Student Identity Development." *Journal of Gay and Lesbian Issues in Education,* 2005, *3*(1).

Carter, K. A. "Transgenderism and College Students: Issues of Gender Identity and Its Role on Our Campuses." In V. A. Wall and N. J. Evans (eds.), *Toward Acceptance: Sexual Orientation Issues on Campus.* Washington, D.C.: American College Personnel Association, 2000.

Coalition for Queer Action. "Queer Action Campaign: Gender-Neutral Bathrooms." 2001. http://www.pissr.org/research.html. Accessed Oct. 15, 2004.

Curtis, B., and Tubbs, N. J. "Housing and Residential Life." In L. Strimpel, K. Mayeda, and R. Sanlo (eds.), *Transactions: Transgender Issues in Student Affairs.* Unpublished manuscript, 2004.

Dean, L. "Lesbian, Gay, Bisexual, and Transgender Health: Findings and Concerns." *Journal of the Gay and Lesbian Medical Association,* 2000, *4*(3), 102–151.

DeBerard, M. S., Spielmans, G., and Julka, D. "Predictors of Academic Achievement and Retention Among College Freshmen: A Longitudinal Study." *College Student Journal,* 2004, *38*(1), 66.

Ettner, R., and Brown, G. *Gender Loving Care: A Guide to Counseling Gender Variant Clients.* New York: Norton, 1999.

Feldman, J., and Bockting, W. "Transgender Health." *Minnesota Medicine,* 2003, *86,* 25–32. http://www.mnmed.org/publications/MNMed2003/July/Feldman.html. Accessed Oct. 15, 2004.

FTM Alliance of Los Angeles. *Results of the 2003 Health Access Survey: The Female-to-Male Transgender Community Experiences Multiple Barriers to Healthcare in Southern California.* Los Angeles: FTM Alliance, 2004.

Gender Identity Working Group. *Final Report of the Gender Identity Working Group,* 6/23/03. Ann Arbor: University of Michigan, 2003.

Gould, D. "Counseling Services: Counseling Issues with Transgender and Gender Variant Students." In L. Strimpel, K. Mayeda, and R. Sanlo (eds.), *Transactions: Transgender Issues in Student Affairs.* Unpublished manuscript, 2004.

Harry Benjamin International Gender Dysphoria Association. "The HBIGDA Standards of Care for Gender Identity Disorders, Sixth Version." 2001. http://www.hbigda.org/soc.cfm. Accessed Oct. 15, 2004.

Israel, G., and Tarver, D. E., II. *Transgender Care: Recommended Guidelines, Practical Information, and Personal Accounts.* Philadelphia: Temple University Press, 1997.

Lees, L. J. "Transgender Students on Our Campuses." In R. L. Sanlo (ed.), *Working with Lesbian, Gay, Bisexual, and Transgender College Students: A Handbook for Faculty and Administrators*. Westport, Conn.: Greenwood Press, 1998.

Lombardi, E., and Davis, S. "Transgender Health Issues." In D. F. Morrow and L. Messinger (eds.), *Sexual Orientation and Gender Identity in Social Work Practice*. New York: Columbia University Press, forthcoming.

Matney, M. *Gender Identity Group Student Survey Results*. Ann Arbor: University of Michigan, 2003.

McKinney, J. "On the Margins: A Study of the Experiences of Transgender College Students." *Journal of Gay and Lesbian Issues in Education*, 2005, 3(1).

Nakamura, K. "Transitioning on Campus: A Case Studies Approach." In R. L. Sanlo (ed.), *Working with Lesbian, Gay, Bisexual, and Transgender College Students: A Handbook for Faculty and Administrators*. Westport, Conn.: Greenwood Press, 1998.

Ohio State University. "OSU Transgender Guide and Resources." 2005. http://multicul-turalcenter.osu.edu/glbtss. Accessed Mar. 28, 2005.

Pusch, R. "Objects of Curiosity: Transgender College Students' Perception of the Reactions of Others." *Journal of Gay and Lesbian Issues in Education*, 2005, 3(1).

Rankin, S. R. *Campus Climate for Gay, Lesbian, Bisexual, and Transgender People: A National Perspective*. New York: National Gay and Lesbian Task Force Policy Institute, 2003.

San Francisco Human Rights Commission. "Gender Neutral Bathroom Survey." 2001. http://www.pissr.org/research.html. Accessed Oct. 15, 2004.

Sausa, L. A. "Updating College and University Campus Policies: Meeting the Needs of Trans Students, Staff, and Faculty." In E. P. Cramer (ed.), *Addressing Homophobia and Heterosexism on College Campuses*. Binghamton, N.Y.: Harrington Park Press, 2002.

Transgender Law and Policy Institute. "Ways that Colleges and Universities Meet the Needs of Transgender Students." http://www.transgenderlaw.org/college/index.htm. Accessed Mar. 15, 2005.

University of California, Berkeley, Health Services. "Services for Transgender Students." 2004. http://www.uhs.berkeley.edu/students/medical/transgender.shtml. Accessed Oct. 15, 2004.

University of California, Riverside. "UCR Housing Policies Related to Gender Identity/Expression." 2005. http://www.out.ucr.edu/transpolicy.html. Accessed March 28, 2005.

University of Michigan Health System Comprehensive Gender Services Program. 2004. http://www.med.umich.edu/transgender. Accessed Oct. 15, 2004.

University of Minnesota Transgender Health Services. 2004. http://www.med.umn.edu/fp/phs/tgs.htm. Accessed Oct. 15, 2004.

Xavier, J. *The Washington Transgender Needs Assessment Survey*. 2000. http://www.glaa.org/archive/2000/tgneedsassessment1112.shtml. Accessed Oct. 15, 2004.

BRETT BEEMYN *is director of the LGBT Center at Ohio State University.*

BILLY CURTIS *is director of the LGBT Center at the University of California, Berkeley.*

MASEN DAVIS *is a social worker and founder and director of the FTM Alliance of Los Angeles.*

NANCY JEAN TUBBS *is director of the LGBT Center at the University of California, Riverside.*

6

Due to the transitory nature of students at community colleges, it is often difficult for student affairs professionals to connect with LGBT students and even more difficult for them to provide services for this invisible population.

LGBT Students in Community College: Characteristics, Challenges, and Recommendations

Brian T. Ivory

In 1967, two years before the Stonewall Riots in New York that are said to have ignited the modern gay civil rights movement, Columbia University became the first campus to recognize a student organization for gay and lesbian students (Mallory, 1998). Four years later, the University of Michigan established the first resource center for lesbian, gay, bisexual, and transgender (LGBT) students. According to the National Consortium of Directors of LGBT Resources in Higher Education (2005), more than one hundred formally staffed resource centers are operating in the United States and Canada. The only LGBT center attributed to a two-year institution is at the Community College of Denver (at Auraria), which is a shared resource center in partnership with Metropolitan State College and the University of Colorado at Denver (National Consortium, 2005).

This trend in LGBT resource centers supports the conventional belief that community colleges have responded more slowly to sexual minority students than have four-year institutions. In fact, since Baker (1991) first called attention to this "invisible minority" at two-year colleges, fewer than six articles have been published regarding this population. Furthermore, recent publications focused on American community colleges (Cohen and Brawer, 2003) and minority populations at two-year colleges (Laden, 2004) are silent on the topic of lesbian, gay, bisexual, and transgender students. Empirical research on LGBT students at community colleges is also "notably absent" in the higher education literature (Leider, 2000).

The fact that community colleges constitute one-third of enrollment in American higher education (Cohen and Brawer, 2003) makes evident the need for LGBT-based research and student services at two-year institutions. The topics selected for this chapter are aimed primarily at student affairs professionals working in community college settings. Barriers to identifying and meeting the needs of LGBT students outside the classroom will be emphasized. For example, the transitory nature of community college students makes it difficult for LGBT persons to connect with other sexual minorities on campus. Also, these topics should interest student personnel staff employed at commuter campuses and educational researchers who wish to study sexual minorities at both types of campuses.

The first section in this chapter addresses the current state of research involving lesbian, gay, bisexual, and transgender students at community colleges. Obstacles to studying a campus population "that may not wish to be identified" (Leider, 1999, p. 2) will also be discussed.

Obstacles to Researching Sexual Minorities at Community Colleges

In a review of the literature regarding two-year institutions, Leider (1999) discovered that studies on LGBT students were practically nonexistent: "Given the state of current research in the field, it is not overstating the case to say that we know virtually nothing about LGBT students on community college campuses" (p. 15). For example, he found no studies that attempted to quantify the number of sexual minorities at either two-year colleges or four-year institutions. Therefore, Leider concludes, "the extent to which this student population exists on community college campuses can only be surmised" (1999, p. 1).

To provide a context for this lack of research, Leider (1999, 2000) points out several obstacles to studying lesbian, gay, bisexual, and transgender students. For example, Leider (2000) notes that sexual minorities are often reluctant to identify themselves, partly due to the social stigma associated with sexuality labels, and partly due to the fact that some LGBT students may reject being labeled altogether. In addition, LGBT students in the early stages of the coming-out process may not be in a position to self-identify with any particular sexual orientation or gender identity: "Consequently, any examination of this special population can yield only a partial picture" (Leider, 1999, p. 2).

Just as no empirical studies have been conducted regarding the campus experiences of LGBT students attending community colleges, neither have specific data been collected from sexual minorities regarding the prevalence of antigay violence and harassment at two-year institutions. Leider (2000) claims this particular area of research is complicated by the fact that many LGBT students fail to report antigay crime and harassment to authorities on campus. His suggestion that antigay hate crimes are underreported at community colleges is supported in the higher education literature on four-year institutions (see, for example, Bieschke, Eberz, and Wilson, 2000; Downey and Stage, 1999; Franklin, 1998).

According to Leider (1999, 2000), one researcher's response to this problem was to focus on the perpetrators of antigay violence and harassment rather than their victims. Franklin's (1998) innovative study involving a diverse sample of community college students produced some indirect insights into the lives of LGBT students at two-year institutions. For example, one out of every three undergraduates in that study reported committing hate crimes or hate speech against those presumed to be homosexual. Additional insights gained from Franklin's study will be explored in the following section focused on campus safety issues for LGBT students.

Safety Issues: Antigay Violence and Harassment on the Two-year Campus

The prevalence of antigay violence and harassment is a growing concern within the higher education community (Leider, 2000). Based on research involving four-year institutions, Bieschke, Eberz, and Wilson (2000) concluded that sexual minorities are more likely than heterosexual students to be the victims of verbal harassment, physical assault, intimidation, and discrimination. A recent national campus climate survey conducted by Rankin (2003) supports this conclusion. Rankin surveyed nearly seventeen hundred LGBT students, faculty, and staff at four-year colleges and universities. Her findings indicate that, within the previous year, more than one-third of sexual minorities had experienced antigay harassment on campus. In addition, 20 percent of respondents feared for their physical safety, while another 51 percent concealed their sexual or gender identity to avoid antigay intimidation.

As for studies involving two-year institutions, Franklin's survey (1998) of 484 community college students regarding antigay aggression indicates the "rate of antigay violence among these young adults was truly alarming" (p. 2). For example, her findings reveal that one in ten respondents admitted to physical violence or threats against people they presumed were gay men or lesbians. An additional 24 percent of study participants reported name-calling toward individuals presumed to be homosexual. Furthermore, the majority of undergraduates in this study acknowledged having either participated in or witnessed antigay incidents.

Since no research has been conducted involving LGBT students at two-year institutions (Leider, 2000), the prevalence of antigay violence and harassment can only be surmised. Citing the Franklin 1998 study, Leider (2000) concluded that antigay hate crimes and hate speech on two-year campuses is far more widespread than previously thought: "While we know little about these students, we do know that they are being subjected to harassment and hate crimes by their peers. . . . It is clear that LGBT community college students have a set of needs that are clamoring for attention" (p. 4).

The following section will explore the barriers—campus environments that are hostile toward sexual minorities—that can hinder the identity development and coming-out process of LGBT students enrolled at community colleges.

Challenges to Fostering an LGBT Sexual Identity Formation

Student development is a primary function for student affairs professionals at community colleges as well as at four-year institutions (Leider, 1999). According to Leider (1999), student services, activities, and programs are typically informed by theories delineating those developmental tasks common to traditional-age college students (see, for example, Chickering and Reisser, 1993). Lesbian, gay, bisexual, and transgender students undergo an additional sexual or gender-identity formation process (Leider, 1999). Cass (1979) provided the first theoretical framework regarding the stages of development associated with homosexual identity formation. According to Leider (2000), it is now common for LGBT students to arrive at community colleges "already at some stage of this developmental process and seeking the services of student affairs professionals" (p. 3).

For LGBT students, coming out is a major aspect in the process of sexual identity formation (von Destinon, Evans, and Wall, 2000). According to Bieschke, Eberz, and Wilson (2000), this process "seems to begin with a period of self-acknowledgement followed by selective disclosure to others" (p. 52). However, these authors note, LGBT students may engage in efforts to disguise or conceal their sexual identities, especially when they feel threatened. To avoid antigay violence and harassment, LGBT students will often attempt to pass as heterosexuals (Baker, 1991). Such closeted strategies are generally regarded as antithetical to developing a positive sexual or gender identity (Leck, 1998).

Once again, published research and related literature are unavailable regarding the sexual-identity development of LGBT students at community colleges. Hence, the following insights are drawn from Leck's article (1998) on sexual minorities enrolled at commuter campuses. As a long-term LGBT faculty advisor, Leck (1998) offered her perceptions regarding the issues and concerns facing this student population—insights that are most applicable to LGBT students attending two-year colleges.

With regard to sexual identity development, Leck (1998) contends that commuter students face additional challenges compared to their four-year counterparts. For example, she observes that students who leave home to attend larger, residential universities may benefit from greater tolerance, advocacy, and campus programming for the LGBT population. She further notes, "The anonymity a large campus may provide will offer some cover for identity struggles and experimentation that cannot be cultivated on the commuter campus" (p. 378). However, she contends, for commuter college students "who cannot afford to move away from their parents' home the 'escape to freedom' is not easily managed" (p. 374). According to Leck, sexual minorities who remain closeted in the home front often turn to drugs, alcohol, promiscuity, and even suicide for relief from the confusion of heterosexual expectations.

A final challenge to LGBT students fostering their sexual-identity formation involves the visibility of, and connection with, other sexual minorities on campus. According to Bieschke, Eberz, and Wilson (2000), research from four-year colleges suggests that supportive relationships with other LGBT students "appear to be critical for students to develop a positive and proud identity" (p. 52). Hence, barriers to making formal connections with LGBT students, faculty, and staff on community and commuter college campuses is the focus of the next section.

Barriers to Maintaining and Sustaining LGBT Connections on Campus

The first barrier to sexual minority students forming connections on campus is due to the invisible campus population (Baker, 1991). On an informal basis, it can be difficult for LGBT students to identify other sexual minorities on commuter and community college campuses. Even when sexual minorities are visible on campus—such as at a program addressing LGBT concerns—some students may wish to avoid "the risk of public association in their own community" (Leck, 1998, p. 377]). This hesitation is especially true for those students who have yet to disclose their sexual orientation to friends and family of origin.

Another barrier common at these institutions is "commuter campus syndrome," which Leider (1999) defines as behavior "wherein students arrive from off campus, take their classes, and then leave" (p. 6). Both Leck (1998) and Leider (1999) observe that time constraints on LGBT students inhibit their ability to connect with sexual minorities on campus. For example, Leck explains that commuter students typically "work at least twenty hours a week while going to school full-time, or they work full-time and attend school part-time" (1998, p. 379). Other contributions of this barrier include the lack of institutional support services for sexual minorities, the lack of on-campus housing, and the fact that many LGBT students still live at home (Leider, 1999).

Opportunities to interact with LGBT students, faculty, and staff can play a significant role in sexual minority students' ability to persist toward graduation (Leider, 2000). Likewise, Cullen and Smart (1991) note, "Visible and proud gay, lesbian, or bisexual faculty or staff can provide enormous opportunities for students" (p. 185). According to these authors, such opportunities include mentoring and role modeling, through which sexual minority students can better understand their LGBT-related experiences. "If there are no visible gay, lesbian, or bisexual professionals on campus, students may perceive . . . that they are not valued; they may go underground, leave the institution, or, worse yet, not accept who they are" (p. 185). Benefits aside, the presence and availability of LGBT professionals in higher education is generally limited (Kraig, 1998).

In addition to establishing contacts with sexual minorities on campus, many LGBT students will seek out other venues of involvement at community colleges. For example, these students may avail themselves of existing services, campus programs, or LGBT-centered student organizations. Hence, student affairs professionals should be mindful that the often transitory nature of student enrollment at two-year institutions constitutes another barrier to sustaining connections between sexual minorities on campus. (Weiss, 2004–2005). In other words, the students at community colleges vary in terms of sustained enrollment, sporadic enrollments, and permanent departure from campus.

Nowhere is this challenge more evident than with LGBT-centered student organizations. According to Outcalt (1998), sexual-minority groups at every college or university must find ways to sustain member involvement and group effectiveness. One particular challenge involves recruiting a "critical mass" (p. 332) needed for various leadership roles within an LGBT student organization. As a long-time advisor to LGBT groups, Leck (1998) discovered that each new student organization "lasted two to four years, usually until the founding members graduated and left the campus" (p. 376). Given the transitory nature of community college enrollment, fostering long-term continuity within LGBT-centered groups is especially difficult.

The final section of this chapter offers recommendations for educational researchers and personnel working with LGBT students in community college settings.

Recommendations for Educational Researchers and Student Affairs Professionals

The research for this chapter illuminated several concerns regarding the existing research and literature on sexual minorities at two-year institutions. First, it is alarming that no empirical studies have been conducted on this LGBT population. In fact, Leider (1999) declares "there is so little research regarding LGBT student[s], faculty, and staff on community college campuses that any research in the field will be a contribution" (p. 15). Second, fewer than six publications are available regarding the characteristics and campus experiences of LGBT students at two-year colleges. This lack of knowledge is especially problematic for student affairs professionals wishing to draw from the higher education literature to plan LGBT programs and services at community colleges.

According to Bieschke, Eberz, and Wilson (2000), additional research is "essential to further our understanding of this often invisible and frequently unacknowledged population" (p. 50). Despite the difficulty of studying LGBT students, these authors provide a useful research agenda that includes methodological guidelines and suggested study questions. Since their agenda fails to address topics of inquiry specific to community colleges, the following additional research questions are provided:

In what ways is the sexual identity formation of LGBT students at community colleges similar to or different from that of sexual minorities at four-year institutions?

How does living at home or within one's home town affect the coming-out process of LGBT students at two-year colleges? In addition, how do these characteristics affect their engagement with LGBT persons, programs, and services on campus?

What are the unique characteristics and challenges of nontraditional sexual-minority students (specifically, those twenty-five years or older)?

What are the unique characteristics and challenges of LGBT students of color?

To conclude this chapter, recommendations for student affairs professionals are provided with regard to three topics: campus safety issues, identity development of sexual minorities, and off-campus referrals to community agencies and resources.

According to von Destinon, Evans, and Wall (2000), it remains "the responsibility of institutions and student affairs personnel to support, encourage, and protect students, regardless of sexual orientation" (p. 385). However, empirical research conducted by Rankin (2003) and Franklin (1998) indicates that antigay crimes and harassment are prevalent at both community colleges and four-year institutions. To increase campus safety for LGBT populations, institutional leaders at two-year colleges are encouraged to adopt nondiscrimination policies or diversity statements that speak to sexual orientation and gender identity. Such campus policies should also be disseminated to students via admissions materials, student handbooks, college catalogues, and orientation handouts. Furthermore, Evans and Wall (2000) contend that "student affairs staff must see that these policies are strictly enforced" (p. 394). Finally, the specific steps for reporting antigay crimes to campus and local authorities should be communicated to all students, faculty, and staff.

While fostering the inclusion of sexual minorities is ultimately an "institutional affair" (Ottenritter, 1998), student affairs professionals are often responsible for coordinating LGBT-related programs and services. With regard to sexual-minority students, Evans and Wall (2000) place special importance on the developmental needs of this population: "Fostering human growth and development needs to be the foundation upon which all student affairs programs and services are built" (p. 393). In other words, the work of the profession involves promoting educational environments and experiences that may facilitate LGBT students' sexual-identity development. With this in mind, student personnel workers should remain attentive to the needs of sexual minorities, particularly in admissions and retention services, student life programming, student organizations, campus governance, counseling services, health centers, and public safety departments.

In cases where the needs of LGBT persons cannot be met through existing resources, off-campus referrals to community programs and agencies become indispensable. According to Leck (1998), building relationships "with local social service agencies and religious services are of utmost importance, because they provide connections for intergroup support among LGBT people" (p. 380). Therefore, institutional relationships with local referral sites become critical to the well-being of lesbian, gay, bisexual, and transgender students. In some cases, such as posting flyers for the local crisis hotline, connecting LGBT students with an appropriate agency may be a matter of life or death. In addition, student affairs professionals should maintain resource areas around campus where sexual-minority students can gather information about community agencies, programs, and services.

References

Baker, J. A. "Gay Nineties: Addrsssing the Needs of the Homosexual Community and Junior College Students and Faculty." *Community/Junior College,* 1991, *15*(1), 25–32.

Bieschke, K. J., Eberz, A. B., and Wilson, D. "Empirical Investigations of the Gay, Lesbian, and Bisexual College Student." In V. A. Wall, and N. J. Evans (eds.), *Toward Acceptance: Sexual Orientation Issues on Campus.* Washington, D.C.: American College Personnel Association, 2000.

Cass, V. C. "Homosexual Identity Formation: A Theoretical Model." *Journal of Homosexuality,* 1979, *4,* 219–235.

Chickering, A. W., and Reisser, L. *Education and Identity.* San Francisco: Jossey-Bass, 1993.

Cohen, A. M., and Brawer, F. B. *The American Community College.* San Francisco: Jossey-Bass, 2003.

Cullen, M., and Smart, J. "Issues of Gay, Lesbian, and Bisexual Student Affairs Professionals." In N. J. Evans and V. A. Wall (eds.), *Beyond Tolerance: Gays, Lesbians and Bisexuals on Campus.* Washington, D.C.: American College Personnel Association, 1991.

Downey, J. P., and Stage, F. K. "Hate Crimes and Violence on College and University Campuses." *Journal of College Student Development,* 1999, *40*(1), 3–9.

Evans, N. J., and Wall, V. A. "Parting Thoughts: An Agenda for Addressing Sexual Orientation Issues on Campus." In V. A. Wall and N. J. Evans (eds.), *Toward Acceptance: Sexual Orientation Issues on Campus.* Washington, D.C.: American College Personnel Association, 2000.

Franklin, K. "Psychological Motivations of Hate Crimes Perpetrators: Implications for Educational Intervention." Paper presented at the 106th Annual Convention of the American Psychological Association, San Francisco, 1998. (ED 423 939)

Kraig, B. "Faculty and Staff Mentors for LGBT Students: Key Responsibilities and Requirements." In R. L. Sanlo (ed.), *Working with Lesbian, Gay, Bisexual, and*

Transgender College Students: A Handbook for Faculty and Administrators. Westport, Conn.: Greenwood Press, 1998.

Laden, B. V. (ed.). *Serving Minority Populations.* New Directions for Community Colleges, no. 127. San Francisco: Jossey-Bass, 2004.

Leck, G. M. "An Oasis: The LGBT Student Group on a Commuter Campus." In R. L. Sanlo (ed.), *Working with Lesbian, Gay, Bisexual, and Transgender College Students: A Handbook for Faculty and Administrators.* Westport, Conn.: Greenwood Press, 1998.

Leider, S. "Sexual Minorities on Community College Campuses." Los Angeles: ERIC Clearinghouse for Community Colleges, 1999. (ED 447 841)

Leider, S. "Sexual Minorities on Community College Campuses." Los Angeles: ERIC Clearinghouse for Community Colleges, 2000. (ED 427 796).

Mallory, S. "Lesbian Gay, Bisexual, and Transgender Student Organizations: An Overview." In R. L. Sanlo (ed.), *Working with Lesbian, Gay, Bisexual, and Transgender College Students: A Handbook for Faculty and Administrators.* Westport, Conn.: Greenwood Press, 1998.

National Consortium of Directors of LGBT Resources in Higher Education. 2005. http://www.lgbtcampus.org. Accessed Jan. 12, 2005.

Ottenritter, N. "The Courage to Care: Addressing Sexual Minority Issues on Campus." In American Association of Community Colleges (ed.), *Removing Vestiges: Research-Based Strategies to Promote Inclusion.* Washington, D.C.: American Association of Community Colleges, 1998.

Outcalt, C. "The Life Cycle of LGBT Organizations: Finding Ways to Sustain Involvement and Effectiveness." In R. L. Sanlo (ed.), *Working with Lesbian, Gay, Bisexual, and Transgender College Students: A Handbook for Faculty and Administrators.* Westport, Conn.: Greenwood Press, 1998.

Rankin, S. *Campus Climate for Gay, Lesbian, Bisexual and Transgender People: A National Perspective.* New York: National Gay and Lesbian Task Force Policy Institute, 2003.

Von Destinon, M., Evans, N., and Wall, V. A. "Navigating the Minefield: Sexual Orientation Issues and Campus Politics." In V. A. Wall and N. J. Evans (eds.), *Toward Acceptance: Sexual Orientation Issues on Campus.* Washington, D.C.: American College Personnel Association, 2000.

Weiss, D. F. "Community College Freshmen: Last In, Last Out?" *Journal of College Student Retention: Research, Theory and Practice,* 2004–2005, 6(2).

BRIAN T. IVORY *is a counselor and assistant professor in counseling and student development at Mott Community College, Flint, Michigan.*

There are many ways in which a campus LGBT office or center can be established. This chapter tells the story of one institution's journey to creating such a center and the tools used to make that creation happen.

The Evolution of an LGBT Center at a Public Institution

Robin Ryan

Since 1971 Oregon State University (OSU) has developed a history of supporting students by providing recruitment, retention, and education programs for underrepresented communities. Four cultural centers, a women's center, and four minority education offices provide education, safe space, advocacy, and community for students, staff, and faculty at OSU. The four cultural centers—Native American Longhouse, Lonnie B. Harris Black Cultural Center, Asian Pacific Cultural Center, and Centro Cultural Cesar Chavez—operate from four freestanding homes located throughout the campus. As programs funded by student fees, with average annual budgets of $44,000, these centers are run by students for students. The existence and success of the centers paved the way for student leaders from the lesbian, gay, bisexual, transgender (LGBT), and ally student organization, along with the director of the lesbian, gay, and bisexual task force and representatives from the student government, to voice their dream of creating a center for the LGBT community during winter term 2000.

With the goal of establishing a safe gathering place for LGBT students, these student leaders spent six months developing a vision based on the model of the existing cultural centers. At the request of the students, the Student Involvement Diversity Development office, the budget source for the other centers, agreed to add $7,000 to its student fee budget request for 2001–2002 to support the start-up operational and personnel costs of an LGBT program.

During winter term, the student fee funding process provided the OSU community with a forum that exhibited how divided the student body was about creating a center for LGBT students. Individual students representing all factions of campus, including religious organizations, political organizations, student government, and cultural centers, gave voice to the debate. Some students openly voiced concern over having LGBT individuals trying to achieve the same status and services as students of color and ethnic minorities on campus. After weeks of community dialogues and hundreds of letters to the editor of the student newspaper, the student fee committee heard the budget request. Three hundred and fifty individuals, opponents and supporters alike, contributed to an hour-long, heated discussion ending in a unanimous seven to zero vote in favor of the $7,000 budget. After months of being on the frontlines of the oftentimes hateful dialogues, the LGBT students had hope and funding to proceed with the development of a plan to establish a Queer Resource Center (QRC) on the OSU campus.

The Student Involvement office worked with the students to identify the next steps for the project. The first priority was to establish a temporary space for the students to work in. In the fall of 2001, a small office in the Women's Center, a Student Involvement program housed in a freestanding building in the center of campus, became the location for the QRC. The QRC moved forward as a smaller version of the OSU cultural centers. As in all of the OSU centers, two students led the development of the program in the roles of internal and external coordinators. The internal coordinator focused on the development of information, resources, and programs, and the external coordinator focused on moving the discussion forward about a permanent location and long-term goals for the program. Identifying the importance of community involvement to both internal programming and external development, the students quickly moved on creating an advisory board. The advisory board (made up of students, staff, faculty, and community members) committed to continuing the development of the center by researching a permanent location, supporting the student staff, and identifying community resources and service providers. During that first year, the QRC sponsored social and educational events and provided information and community for hundreds of students.

In the second year of the Center (2002–2003) the student staff, supported by members of the advisory board and the LGBT community, set out to assess the community needs for an LGBT program. This group identified the *Lesbian, Gay, Bisexual, and Transgender Programs and Services Guidelines: Self Assessment Guide* from the Council for the Advancement of Standards in Higher Education (CAS, 2001) as the only tool available to assist in this process. Examination of the guide indicated that the current student-fee-funded and student-run center, although a good beginning, did not meet the suggested standards. In fact, none of the suggested thirteen elements— mission, program, leadership, organization and management, human resources, financial resources, facilities, technology, and equipment, legal responsibilities, equity and access, campus and eternal relations, diversity, ethics, assessment, and evaluation—could be measured because none were in place. The need for a partnership between students and the university to create a comprehensive LGBT program became clear. The assessment committee created a proposal requesting the development of an LGBT program as a component of the permanent QRC that would be in line with CAS (2001), with hopes of gaining university commitment in dollars and other support.

About the same time, the university was working on diversity issues as a component of a campuswide assessment and planning process dubbed OSU-2007. The "2007" Diversity Committee findings suggested developing a program to support the LGBT community based on the models of the OSU Minority Education Offices: Asian/Pacific American Education Office, Casa Education Office, Indian Education Office, and Ujima Education Office. These were programs that focused on the recruitment and retention of underrepresented students. They were run by professional faculty with staff and student support and housed in the OSU administration building.

Both the assessment committee and the 2007 committee submitted their proposals to the Vice Provost for Student Affairs, Larry Roper, shifting what had begun as a student initiative to a joint venture between administration and students. A small group of students and administrative staff then sifted through the reports to create a strategic plan for moving forward. The university committed to providing resources for hiring an LGBT Program Coordinator, developing a comprehensive LGBT services program, and making available a permanent space for the QRC.

The QRC external coordinator and the QRC advisory board continued to focus on securing a permanent location, working with administrators from facilities, public safety, and housing. The ideal location would provide access for people with disability; allow office space for student and professional staff; and have meeting space, kitchen facilities, and lounge space. The collaborative efforts led to identifying a location in fall 2003.

The students presented a funding request through the student fee committee for $120,000 from a reserve account to remodel, furnish, and equip the space. Once again, after some debate, the student fee committee and the student senate approved the funding.

Vice Provost Roper worked with the LGBT community to create a position description for an LGBT coordinator and a program budget for LGBT services. Working closely with the Queer Resource Center, the coordinator, as professional faculty, would be responsible for developing the student staff of the center while creating a campuswide program focused on education, recruitment, retention, and support of LGBT students.

On National Coming Out Day, October 11, 2004, Oregon State University held the grand opening of the OSU Pride Center, the permanent replacement of the Queer Resource Center and the home for LGBT services on the campus. Hundreds of supporters celebrated the addition of the center to the OSU community. A component of student life, the center has a full-time coordinator for LGBT services, two student coordinators, and a small student staff. The Pride Center provides programs and resources for lesbian, gay, bisexual, transgender, queer, questioning, and intersex (LGBTQQIA) members of the OSU community and their allies. The center affirms LGBTQQIA identities and lives by providing education, trained peer support, outreach, community development, visibility, and advocacy. It offers a safe space for all people to learn about and become familiar with many aspects and issues of sexual orientation and gender identity.

This accomplishment, though not an easy one, is an example of how communities can provide a safe, supportive living and learning environment for all students. The Oregon State University mission statement states, "We value diversity because it enhances our education and provides tools to be culturally respectful, professionally competent, and civically responsible." Expressing this value is an ongoing, living process on the OSU campus, honoring students' passions, identifying and assessing needs, and committing people and resources, as seen with the initiative that led to the development of OSU's comprehensive LGBT services program.

Reference

Council for the Advancement of Standards in Higher Education (CAS). *Lesbian, Gay, Bisexual, and Transgender Programs and Services Guidelines: Self Assessment Guide,* Washington D.C.: CAS, 2001.

ROBIN RYAN *is a member of the ORC/Pride Center advisory board and the faculty advisor to the Rainbow Continuum, the LGBT student organization at Oregon State University.*

The authors address the need for including LGBT issues in student affairs graduate education, sharing current practices in select graduate programs and recommending a model for best practice.

Incorporating LGBT Issues into Student Affairs Graduate Education

D. M. Talbot, Wanda L. E. Viento

The presence of students who identify as lesbian, gay, bisexual, or transgender (LGBT) and the issues and needs these students face because of ignorance and discrimination have been established in earlier chapters of this volume. The goal of this chapter is to challenge student affairs professionals and faculty to examine our curricula and make revisions if necessary in order to provide training for future practitioners who will be working with LGBT students across our campuses.

We need no longer debate whether we should be providing education and training around LGBT issues. Both the National Association of Student Personnel Administrators (NASPA) and the American College Personnel Association (ACPA) have clear indicators in their standards and ethical codes regarding issues on diversity and specifically highlighting LGBT students and issues (http://www.naspa.org, http://www.acpa.nche.edu). In addition, the curriculum guidelines set out by the Council for the Advancement of Standards in Higher Education (CAS) also include clear statements about the inclusion of sexual minorities in student affairs graduate education (http://www.cas.edu). Therefore, the only questions left are: How do we best educate our professionals and when will this change take place in the majority of our master's and doctoral programs?

Calling for curriculum changes to infuse diversity issues into graduate training programs, specifically including content on LGBT issues, is not new (see, for example, Evans and Wall, 1991; Newman, 1989; Wall and Evans, 2000). In the landmark student affairs publication *Beyond Tolerance: Gays, Lesbians, and Bisexuals on Campus*, Evans and Wall (1991) sent a wake-up

New Directions for Student Services, no. 111, Fall 2005 © Wiley Periodicals, Inc.

call to the profession. They declared that in order "to address the needs of gay, lesbian, and bisexual students, student affairs professionals must educate themselves about the issues faced by this population" (p. xiv). Yet in their 1997 study on the diversity emphasis in graduate student affairs programs, Talbot and Kocarek found that faculty would take more initiative, and were more comfortable, learning (and teaching) about women and people of color than about LGBT people. While there has been an increase in diversity-related trainings and classes developed in graduate programs (Flowers, 2003), the lack of inclusion of LGBT issues is still evident, as reflected in research on faculty members' and practitioners' knowledge, skills, and behaviors around these issues (Croteau and Lark, 1995; Talbot and Kocarek, 1997). Clearly, educating ourselves has not been successful, or at least not a priority.

What We Know and What's Being Done

In an informal review of titles of courses required in several student affairs graduate curricula, Sanlo (2002) found none that focused specifically on sexual orientation or gender identity issues. In a national study of diversity requirements in student affairs programs, Flowers (2003) found that 74 percent of institutions required one multicultural class at the master's level, and 8 percent were in the process of adding one. There are no data, though, on what is included in those required diversity courses. Flowers recommended that "adequate time be given in the diversity course to all distinct cultural groups on campus" (p. 78). However, as with many other aspects of diversity, inclusion of LGBT issues may depend on the knowledge and comfort of individual faculty members teaching the course.

Flowers (2003) speculated that integrative approaches (that is, addressing diversity in courses across the curriculum) might inadvertently have negative unintended consequences, such as including race but not sexual orientation. Some assert that programs that are silent on LGBT issues perpetuate homophobia and heterosexism (Chestnut, 1998) and implicitly violate the standards and ethics of NASPA and ACPA.

One crucial aspect of working toward modifying discriminatory practices is recognizing them. This often involves a process in which students confront their own belief systems. Buhrke (1989) suggested that students can become aware of and sensitive to their own homophobic ideas only if they are given adequate opportunity to explore these issues. This cannot be accomplished through a one-time exploration, but must occur in a planned approach, including both singular classes and an integrated curriculum: singular multicultural classes that include LGBT issues, special issues classes focused specifically on LGBT concerns, and the inclusion of LGBT considerations into all student affairs courses. With a curriculum that normalizes the inclusion of LGBT concerns, students will be better prepared to provide services across the board in student affairs.

Many examples of methods to achieve this approach are available. For example, in some curricula, LGBT issues are included in classes specific to theory, legal issues in higher education, introductory counseling, student affairs administration, career and life planning, campus environment, college students and cultures, and practice seminars and internships. More in-depth exploration also occurs in courses on college student development, gender and equity, advanced counseling techniques, and sexuality studies. We also suggest the conscious inclusion of LGBT issues in administrative courses to address the institutional aspects of homophobia and heterosexism. For example, one institution offers a class entitled "Homophobia in Education."

Another approach some institutions are exploring is to offer a series of elective classes or seminars, some specifically focusing on LGBT issues. Other programs have supported students and research by encouraging doctoral dissertations and master's theses that explore various aspects of LGBT themes. On campuses with safe zone–type programs, student affairs students are participating in the training provided for ally development, and panel presentations are used in student affairs classes with LGBT folk sharing their coming-out stories and helping to facilitate discussions.

One faculty member described how she used the play *The Laramie Project* in class to get at the affective component of addressing LGBT issues. She used one full class session in which students read the play aloud, then discussed how it felt to say and hear many of the offensive things that are included in the play. In addition, in-class role-plays are used to explore diversity within the LGBT populations, including gender issues (Whitman, 1995), as well as to help students develop empathy for others' experiences.

As with most areas of diversity training in student affairs, faculty members receive little guidance and few models for incorporating LGBT issues into the curriculum. Well-meaning educators implement efforts such as those listed above on an ad hoc basis, as if there are no parallel models to give direction to our thinking in this area. Yet, if we recognize the dynamic nature of diversity in our world and the importance of student affairs practitioners' being able to assist higher education in providing a safe learning environment for all students, we need to design a flexible curriculum that readily incorporates different populations as the need arises.

Recommendations for Student Affairs Graduate Education Regarding LGBT Issues

In many respects, designing an appropriate student affairs curriculum regarding LGBT issues can be modeled after our vision of multicultural education in general. There should be several components incorporating what we know about how individuals struggle with, and best learn about, diversity. A flexible curriculum must both infuse LGBT issues throughout the curriculum and offer a stand-alone, focused course.

Infusing LGBT issues throughout the curriculum helps to normalize the presence of a population and provides constant reminders about paying attention to LGBT students and issues as individuals learn about the student affairs profession. We also believe that LGBT issues must be included in the single multicultural course that seems to be required in many or most student affairs graduate programs. Instead of perceiving this addition as diffusing the focus of the diversity course, we view this survey course on multicultural populations as a way to allow students to enter the dialogue on diversity where they are most comfortable. Clearly, an underlying assumption with this approach is that the roots of oppression and discrimination are tied together, and that we can learn a process for unlearning our "isms." Therefore, the goal in a survey course that focuses on multiculturalism is to expose students to a variety of topics and populations, including issues of privilege and power, so that they may begin to learn the process for developing a nondiscriminatory and more accepting worldview.

Following this multicultural survey course, graduate programs should offer a rotation of more focused courses, one of which would address LGBT issues, from which students would need to select two or three as part of a diversity cognate. Finally, a focus on diversity and equity would be a required component of the supervised work experience (practicum or internship), with attention given to policies and practices, assessment of environments, and information about students who identify as LGBT. This could then be one of the areas students choose as a component of their field experience.

Conclusion

Although we have suggested an ideal comprehensive model for infusing LGBT issues, as well as other multicultural issues, into graduate student affairs preparation, we are not naive to the challenges this process involves. First, as Talbot and Kocarek (1997) found in their study, graduate faculty address only diversity issues with which they are comfortable and knowledgeable. Since many of our more senior faculty completed their graduate education before LGBT issues were openly recognized, continuing education will be necessary for this group. Yet, faculty struggle to balance a need for their own continuing education—and revamping syllabi accordingly—with demands of systems that do not reward this type of activity. Also, changing or adding to the curriculum often involves a tedious institutional process that faculty find both time-consuming and frustrating.

Second, one of the challenges graduate programs face is the need to incorporate more content into the curriculum without adding credit hours. This is the faculty version of doing more with less, a seemingly impossible task. The goal should be to find a way to make the inclusion of diversity a more seamless process throughout the curriculum, a more naturally integrated part of our philosophy on professional practice.

Finally, institutional cultures may overtly or covertly discourage the inclusion of LGBT issues into the curriculum. Negotiating these political landmines may be perceived as damaging to the careers of nontenured faculty.

In the face of these challenges, why would faculty incorporate LGBT issues into graduate education in student affairs? First, these faculty are responsible for preparing many future student affairs professionals. If our campuses are to be more inviting environments for all students, student affairs professionals must be equipped to design the services and programs that meet the needs of all students. This means that student affairs professionals need appropriate training and education. Second, our professional standards and ethical codes, as well as CAS guidelines, require faculty to attend to diversity issues in developing and delivering their curriculum. To be credible as well as ethical, faculty and graduate programs must model the values that the student affairs profession endorses. Finally, it is the right thing to do. Ultimately, the overall work of the student affairs profession is about inclusion, access, and advocacy for students in higher education. Given this lofty goal, it seems only natural that the student affairs graduate curriculum should include and infuse issues that are important to a population that is marginalized most often in higher education: LGBT students.

References

Buhrke, R. A. "Incorporating Lesbian and Gay Issues into Counselor Training: A Resource Guide." *Journal of Counseling and Development,* 1989, *68,* 77–80.

Chestnut, S. "Queering the Curriculum, or What's Walt Whitman Got to Do with It?" In Sanlo, R. L. (ed.), *Working with Lesbian, Gay, Bisexual, and Transgender College Students: A Handbook for Faculty and Administrators.* Westport, Conn.: Greenwood Press, 1998.

Council for the Advancement of Standards in Higher Education (CAS). *Lesbian, Gay, Bisexual, and Transgender Programs and Services: Standards and Guidelines.* Washington D.C.: CAS, 2001.

Croteau, J. M., and Lark, J. S. "A Qualitative Investigation of Biased and Exemplary Student Affairs Practice Concerning Lesbian, Gay, and Bisexual Issues." *Journal of College Student Development,* 1995, *36,* 472–482.

Evans, N. J., and Wall, V. A. (eds.). *Beyond Tolerance: Gays, Lesbians, and Bisexuals on Campus.* Washington, D.C.: American College Personnel Association, 1991.

Flowers, L. A. "National Study of Diversity Requirements in Student Affairs Graduate Programs." *NASPA Journal,* 2003, *40,* 72–82.

Newman, B. S. "Including Curriculum Content on Lesbian and Gay Issues." *Journal of Social Work Education,* 1989, *2,* 202–211.

Sanlo, R. L. "Scholarship in Student Affairs: Thinking Outside the Triangle, or Tabasco on Cantaloupe." *NASPA Journal,* 2002, *39,* 166–180.

Talbot, D. M., and Kocarek, C. "Student Affairs Graduate Faculty Members' Knowledge, Comfort, and Behaviors Regarding Issues of Diversity." *Journal of College Student Development,* 1997, *38,* 278–287.

Wall, V. A., and Evans, N. J. (eds.). *Toward Acceptance: Sexual Orientation Issues on Campus.* Washington, D.C.: American College Personnel Association, 2000.

Whitman, J. S. "Providing Training About Sexual Orientation in Counselor Education." *Counselor Education and Supervision,* 1995, *35,* 168–176.

D. M. TALBOT *is associate professor and coordinator of the student affairs graduate program at Western Michigan University.*

WANDA L. E. VIENTO *is a doctoral candidate in student affairs in higher education at Western Michigan University. She works at Kalamazoo College.*

*As leaders and community builders, senior student
affairs officers face the challenge to end the hostility,
oppression, and invisibility that often characterize the
experiences of LGBT students on college campuses.*

The Role of Senior Student Affairs Officers in Supporting LGBT Students: Exploring the Landscape of One's Life

Larry D. Roper

This chapter offers the author's reflections on his journey to understand and position himself to be a supportive leader of LGBT issues and an ally to LGBT students and colleagues. This personal narrative draws upon my life experiences and nearly thirty years as a practitioner in the student affairs profession. The assertions, philosophy, and leadership imperatives I offer are ones I have imposed on myself and my leadership role because I believe it is through these attitudes, behaviors, and values that I will fulfill my institution's mission and achieve what I have internalized as the core value of student affairs work—to affirm the dignity and humanity of all students.

During my childhood and young adulthood, gays and lesbians were invisible in my community. But while they were invisible, they certainly were not absent; their presence was just not acknowledged. The behaviors I observed in the adults I loved and looked up to suggested that gays and lesbians were people one whispered about; spoke of in vague, masked terms; or ridiculed, abused, and violated because of who and what they were. The world that formed me and shaped my values did not honor, afford humanity to, or bestow dignity on those who were gay. I grew up in a world where gay, lesbian, and bisexual people were invisible, isolated, powerless, and voiceless.

I assume that many of my contemporaries, as well as those who entered the profession before and after me, also grew up in environments that did not prepare them to live in relationship with, and be supportive of, those

NEW DIRECTIONS FOR STUDENT SERVICES, no. 111, Fall 2005 © Wiley Periodicals, Inc.

who are gay, lesbian, bisexual, and transgender (LGBT). While I want to believe that I have grown into a person committed to service, justice, compassion, and love for all people, I must also admit that I have had to struggle mightily to overcome my early socialization, which was generally inadequate for leadership in a multicultural world and completely insufficient to enable me to support LGBT students. While in my childhood the values of social justice and equity were instilled, I received no messages suggesting gays and lesbians were deserving of just and equitable treatment.

My undergraduate college experience mirrored many of the same dynamics as my childhood. Although I received a wonderful and rich liberal arts education delivered by positive and caring people, it lacked any healthy or respectful mention of gays and lesbians. During my college experience my desire to live a life of service was deepened. I knew by the end of my junior year that I wanted to enter the student affairs profession. Because those who mentored and supported me in my preparation for a career in student affairs never suggested to me that I should possess a commitment to serve LGBT students, I embarked on my career journey with no clue that gay and lesbian students would be part of my professional experience. I went on to graduate school ignorant of and blind to the fact that I would have a professional responsibility for LGBT students.

Following my commitment to a career in higher education in 1975, I entered a graduate preparation program with the belief that the graduate experience would provide me with the knowledge and tools necessary for success. I am thankful for the outstanding education I received in my master's program and the opportunity I had to study with faculty who were nationally recognized in the student affairs profession. Nonetheless, my education was incomplete and insufficient in preparing me to understand the lives, experiences, and needs of gay and lesbian students.

I offer this personal chronology to put forward one thought: I entered the student affairs profession ill prepared to lead an institution toward the meaningful inclusion of LGBT students into the life of an educational community. Moreover, I lacked the awareness, skills, or commitment sufficient to be seen as a legitimate supporter of LGBT issues. I assume most people who ascend to the role of senior student affairs officer do so with the challenge of overcoming many of the socialization and leadership liabilities I had.

Personal awareness and openness are key attributes of successful leadership on the part of senior student affairs officers (SSAOs); I believe that awareness is enhanced by exploring the attitudes and values that have shaped our worldview and that influence how we act toward others. Thus, a senior student affairs leader should first explore the landscape of his life to identify incidents and episodes that enhance or impair his ability to lead in a manner that is supportive of LGBT students.

Because of the unique responsibility student affairs professionals have for campus community building, leadership and support from SSAOs is essential if colleges and universities are to provide meaningful support for

LGBT students. The SSAO who seeks to be a successful leader in this area must attend to important leadership dynamics, among them, developing and acting from a coherent philosophy of service to LGBT students; developing the personal capacity to respond to the leadership needs of the organization and the personal needs of LGBT students; and manifesting the competence to lead and participate in community with LGBT students. The effective leader will have a philosophy that embraces service to LGBT students, will commit to developing successful interpersonal skills, and will invest in knowledge and leadership enhancement.

Leadership Philosophy and Service to LGBT Students

The SSAO should anchor herself to a philosophy by which her work will be influenced and judged. The philosophy of the senior student affairs officer not only influences that individual's work but also can represent a major force that influences the energy and activity of the student affairs organization and campus. The leader's philosophy can set the standards for the belief system from which the student affairs organization will operate, set the tone for how decisions are made, determine the nature of decisions made, influence how resources are allocated, shape the activities engaged in by the organization, and guide the programs the organization implements and supports. Because of the powerful role that individual beliefs and philosophy play in the life of an institution, the guiding philosophy of the senior student affairs officer is of great importance to students, faculty, and staff. However, how the leader's philosophy translates into behavior is even more important—a dynamic, internally held philosophy that does not convert into meaningful activity is of little value to the community served by the senior student affairs officer.

The role of the senior student affairs officer is to develop, articulate, and lead by a philosophy that supports the education, well-being, and success of LGBT students. In this regard the SSAO must be able to communicate how his leadership and organization's functioning contribute to the quality of life and educational experience of LGBT students and staff. This role is made more challenging by the tremendous diversity of institutions in which we lead—public, private, and sectarian. Nonetheless, the value for the whole person that is infused in our profession should empower us to embrace a leadership philosophy that honors and supports the needs of LGBT students regardless of institutional context. SSAOs have the responsibility to develop and act from a philosophy of leadership that puts the success and dignity of all students at the center of their work while also respecting the unique mission of their institution.

Because the SSAO is so crucial to the creation of supportive environments for LGBT students, that individual must demonstrate the capacity to speak articulately and consistently about service to LGBT students as an important dimension of the core mission of the student affairs organization, regardless of institutional context. Even more, the leader's philosophy has to translate to meaningful educational outcomes for individual students and the LGBT community on that campus. The role of the senior student affairs officer is to develop, articulate, live, and lead by an educational philosophy that promotes campuswide awareness and support for LGBT students. Our failure to nurture support for LGBT students means those students will receive less educational value from their campus experience than we are capable of providing.

Developing Personal Capacity to Support LGBT Students

Every student affairs leader is responsible for his learning and preparedness to serve LGBT students. If he does not possess the knowledge to support the organization's leadership responsibility, then it is that individual's responsibility to acquire that knowledge. As we seek to increase the effectiveness of our leadership we will need to take risks and show humility to address the places where we are underprepared. For example, when I entered the student affairs profession, I received no education on the needs and experiences of LGBT students, no information was available on gay and lesbian identity development, and the idea of having as students and providing accommodations to transgender students was nowhere on the professional radar of student affairs. We who entered the profession under such circumstances ought to be humble enough to admit what we do not know and take responsibility to ensure that we are competent in areas that influence the success and well-being of LGBT students. For me that meant addressing knowledge and skill deficits and working to acquire the personal competence necessary to be a leader in areas that influence the success and well-being of LGBT students.

Gaining intellectual competence is a fairly easy proposition, as there is now substantial educational support available in the form of conferences, publications, and workshops. The more challenging leadership issue is achieving the competence in interpersonal leadership needed to translate knowledge into relationships and positive organizational dynamics. Among the organizational and personal issues are supporting the presence of LGBT student organizations, creating and supporting professional positions to support the LGBT community, accommodating unique needs of transgendered students and staff, and mentoring and supervising LGBT students, staff, and colleagues.

The SSAO should demonstrate through her relationships and leadership behavior (including hiring and promotions) that LGBT students, faculty, and staff are valued colleagues and community members. The learning necessary to achieve this style of leadership may be more introspective than external in nature. Through personal reflection, leaders can get in touch with important attributes that influence their behavior as leaders and community builders. Essentially, I recommend that every SSAO commit to exploring and addressing what I refer to as the "dimensions of the leader's being." The dimensions of our being influence what we bring to our relationships with others and how effective we are in our leadership roles. In a very practical way, how we position ourselves relative to others influences what we find pleasing, what we are offended by, what we tolerate, and what we are able to embrace. By exploring who we are and how we interact with those with whom we have opportunities to develop relationships, we are better positioned to address potential relationship challenges and enhance our leadership success. The SSAO must have the ability to develop and sustain relationships with a broad range of people, and that same range of people must see the SSAO as one who is easy to approach and with whom they can easily connect. The SSAO needs to be a campus leader in supporting, mentoring, caring for, and honoring LGBT students.

I offer three specific dimensions of the SSAO's personal being (life) to be explored, which I call weight, depth, and breadth. The exploration process involves answering a series of simple but possibly unfamiliar questions. The questions that accompany each of the three dimensions should cause the SSAO to think more deeply about her attitudes, values, and behaviors.

As the leader explores the weight of his being he will consider the following questions:

- What is the heaviness or lightness I bring to relationships?
- How much psychic or emotional weight am I carrying?
- What challenges might others encounter trying to be in a relationship with me?

The SSAO ought to bring a sense of lightness to her relationships and leadership. If the SSAO's issues weigh too heavily, those issues will impede the leader's ability to acknowledge, serve, and create space for others. The leader cannot have too much personal baggage relative to diversity in general and LGBT issues specifically. Specifically, SSAOs must be aware of the emotional and psychic challenges they must overcome in order to be successful leaders of LGBT issues.

When the SSAO explores the breadth of his being, he focuses on exploring the range of his humanity. In effect, the SSAO asks:

- Who am I capable of wrapping my arms around?
- What is the range of people with whom I am capable of being in community?

The SSAO must be able to wrap his arms around and be in community with LGBT students, which means the SSAO should have the ability to fully embrace and expressly care for LGBT students, and LGBT students, faculty, and staff should be in the SSAO's web of relationships. The SSAO should be visible to the campus as one who promotes and embraces the presence and success of LGBT students.

Finally, the SSAO should investigate the depth of her personal being, which involves exploring questions such as these:

- How far am I able to invite others into my life (through sharing my personal experiences)?
- How deeply am able to explore the life and experiences of others?
- How deeply am I able to feel for others?

I believe it is very difficult for leaders to successfully lead and support those for whom she does not experience care and compassion. Senior student affairs officers must be capable of demonstrating to themselves and to others that they care deeply about LGBT students. The senior student affairs officer should be engaged in understanding the depth and magnitude of the LGBT experience. Through exploring his own life experiences, the SSAO will be able to identify aspects of his background that influence the strengths and challenges that he brings to his responsibilities.

The SSAO should model to campus colleagues—through commitment, humility, and risk taking—what it means to take seriously one's responsibility to gain knowledge and interpersonal competence regarding LGBT issues. If we are to support LGBT students, we must engage our heads and our hearts—and transform our leadership—by acquiring knowledge, skills, behaviors, and genuine care for LGBT students so that we can put their needs at the center of our leadership.

Leadership and Community Building

A major role of the SSAO leader is building and supporting campus community. Through her community-building role she will be actively involved in cultivating the kind of environment needed to ensure the safety, full inclusion, and participation of LGBT students in the life of the campus. In this regard, senior student affairs officers are meaning makers and place makers—creating space for and adding strength, power, and substance to campus relationships. Through boundary-spanning leadership, the SSAO should demonstrate that she can foster connections among those who might otherwise be isolated, make audible those who might feel voiceless, bring visibility to the invisible, and create space at the center of the institution's mission for those who might feel marginalized. It is imperative that SSAOs commit to building campus communities that embody structural, psychological, emotional, and social support for LGBT students. Our leadership must be evidenced by support structures that can be seen, touched, and sensed by LGBT students. As community builders we must use the influence of our roles to remove obstacles, lessen challenges, interrupt threats, and dispel myths that restrict opportunities for success for LGBT students. Although community building is not advocacy, it is active ally work—we do not speak for LGBT students; instead we lead in ways that validate the words they speak and support the needs they express. Advocacy often involves the advocate speaking for the other person, whereas allies support the goals and needs of others. As active allies we work to act on the needs of LGBT students.

Because LGBT issues are still a source of conflict on many campuses, the leadership and commitment of the SSAO may become most evident during times of campus controversy. As an ally to LGBT students, the SSAO should gracefully rise above the noise and conflict that can often come in response to the institution's investment in support for LGBT students and maintain focus on how to support the needs of LGBT students while also enhancing the overall health of the campus community. This gracefulness is most easily achieved by focusing on the institution's responsibility to meet each student's needs for safety and inclusion. The role of the SSAO is not to take sides in the midst of campus discord about LGBT issues, but to elevate the institution's mission such that responding to the needs of LGBT students can be seen as activity critical to that mission. The role of the SSAO is to translate conflict into community.

As a community builder, the SSAO ought to be in attendance and fully participating when the LGBT community convenes for the purpose of celebration, sober reflection, or grieving; we must experience the joy and sorrow of the community. LGBT students should be able to count on the SSAO's presence during key events in the growth and development of the LGBT community in order to validate that person as a visible supporter of the community. The SSAO should not be a distant icon; she ought to be identified as a real and committed participant in the life of the LGBT community. The SSAO can participate in the LGBT community as a workshop facilitator, workshop participant, financial sponsor for events, and advisor to LGBT student leaders.

Leadership and community building mean that we seek to influence all aspects of our organization's culture—using the reach of our leadership to influence the living environment, classroom dynamics, and social climate of the campus. Most important, as leaders and community builders we will work persistently to end the cycle of omission, hostility, ignorance, and invisibility that often characterize the experience of LGBT students on college campuses. As community builders, the role of SSAOs is to transform dramatically the world of higher education into one that brings visibility and voice, honor and dignity, security and safety, and support and success to LGBT students. This challenge is best accomplished through transforming our lives and leadership and allowing that transformation to influence the design and performance of our organizations.

Conclusion

Although there was a time when LGBT students were treated as invisible on college and university campuses, such is not the case now at the vast majority of colleges and universities: they are here, they are visible, and they will not disappear, nor should they. Student affairs leadership will be a key factor in promoting the growth of our institutions as we attempt to cultivate positive, living-learning environments for LGBT students. That long and challenging journey to institutional transformation will be enhanced by leaders who are personally invested in student success and possess the qualities necessary to support the needs of LGBT students and the mission of the institution concurrently. I believe the leadership needed from and expected of us will only come about if we do the hard work of overcoming socialization that might keep us from becoming the kinds of leaders our institutions' missions deserve and our students need and expect.

LARRY D. ROPER is vice provost for student affairs and professor of ethnic studies at Oregon State University.

10

This chapter reflects on the simultaneous journeys of two women, one a lesbian and one an ally. One woman is a midlevel manager in student affairs while the other is the executive director of a national association.

Professional Associates: Journeys of Colleagues in Student Affairs

Judith A. Albin, Gwendolyn Jordan Dungy

Judy's Story

When I began my career in student affairs in 1985, I was a resident director in a women's residence hall on a small campus in the foothills of the Blue Ridge Mountains of southern West Virginia. There were some things that I thought I knew. I knew, for example, that I would not stay in this profession. It was merely a stop along the path of my journey, although I had no idea where the journey would end. I just knew that this residence life thing was not for me. I also knew that I would not, could not, ever be out as a lesbian in this field of student affairs and live my life honestly.

I am a long way from that time in those mountains. Ironically, my journey carried me further into student affairs instead of away from it. I spent sixteen years in residence life and am now in my twentieth year as a student affairs professional. Also ironically, I have been an open lesbian in my work for the past seventeen years. Sometimes it was easy; other times, very difficult. One of my most frightening moments was when a colleague approached me to be the NASPA (National Association of Student Personnel Administrators) Region II Gay, Lesbian, and Bisexual (transgender was to be added later) (GLB) Network chair. I remember thinking that she had lost her mind. There was no way I could do this. How could I be out in my profession for my professional association? But she was persistent and I reluctantly gave in. Because she was to be the regional network coordinator, I was confident that I would not be left on my own. I held that position for several years as

NASPA moved from networks to knowledge communities (KC). I was surprised to find, within this regional work, a home where I felt both welcome and valued. The Region II leadership made it clear that LGBT issues were important. I learned much from that experience and built some valued friendships.

As my term as LGBT Network regional chair was about to end, I was asked to take the National LGBT chair position. Now, the regional role was one thing. As a regional representative I could still lay pretty low and get the job done. But the idea of being the national chair was something very different. I would be the person to whom NASPA looked regarding LGBT issues. I would need to build a national network of colleagues, and I would be interacting with professionals from around the country. I would be the person who must advocate for my NASPA LGBT colleagues.

Being a national representative of anyone or anything is a daunting task, but representing a group of traditionally underrepresented folks is downright intimidating. There is a sense of being the only one, a sense that if I don't get the message out and keep that message in the forefront, "we" lose. We continue to stay at the back of the bus, so to speak. I was also afraid of how I would be viewed leading such a group, obviously being a gay professional. The former chair assured me that she would provide guidance if I needed it. Once again, I knew I had a mentor who was willing to hold me up if I needed it. I accepted the position.

As the national chair, I was very lucky to be surrounded by talented colleagues who were both willing and had the courage to step out to create new experiences for NASPA and our members. One of those experiences was the LGBT Summit, a collaborative pre-conference workshop between NASPA and the National Consortium of Directors of LGBT Resources in Higher Education, many of whom are NASPA members. Although the Summit was to be a one-time-only event, in 2000, Gwen Dungy approached me after it enthusiastically saying, "Wow, what a great Summit! You *are* doing that again next year, right?" Of course I gave her an emphatic yes! The Summit is now in its fifth year and has evolved into an Institute. This is one of many examples of how the encouragement that I received as national LGBT chair bolstered my ability to gather others to do extraordinary work for the profession. I was able to go back to the members who were active in the LGBT Knowledge Community and show them that there was real support for our work from the top. NASPA honestly seemed to care about the issues LGBT professionals were facing and showed concern for us as full-fledged members and colleagues.

When my time came to leave as national chair, instead of being relieved, I felt sad. Luckily, just when I thought my NASPA career was ending, I was asked to be the next national director of Knowledge Communities. I had recently taken on a new role in my real job, the one that pays the bills, so I needed to consider whether or not I could make the time. Being the national director meant that I would be a member of the NASPA board of directors.

While I was worried that I wasn't ready to sit on the board, I knew that this was my chance to stay involved with NASPA at a level where I might be able to make a difference and to maintain relationships with colleagues I truly valued. I accepted the appointment.

I must be honest. I was more than a bit concerned. As usual, I was nervous about being an out lesbian. One is never certain how one will be accepted even when past experiences were positive. I assumed that I would be the only openly LGBT person on the board. I was relieved to learn I was not alone when, in casual conversation, another board member talked about his partner. I realized, too, the truth of that board member's observation that people who choose to be on the NASPA board are typically seasoned professionals who, regardless of their personal beliefs, would be professional in their dealings with other board members. He was right. I received a warm welcome and was made to feel a part of the group from the beginning. I appreciated that there were times during meetings when I did not have to be the person who made sure sexual orientation was part of the conversation. Social justice issues are core values of this board specifically and of NASPA in general. This board walked its talk.

While my fears regarding being an out lesbian and being on the board were put to ease, there are certainly areas at which we need to look more closely as an association. We must address why there are not more out senior student affairs officers (SSAOs). When I was the national LGBT Knowledge Community chair, two things happened surrounding this topic: there was a request from the Alice Manicur Symposium for Women Aspiring to be Senior Student Affairs Officers for assistance and a request from the NASPA office to provide an article about out SSAOs. NASPA had received feedback from the previous Manicur Symposium class that the lack of lesbian visibility was a huge void in the training process. With assistance from other colleagues, I forwarded two names of women interested in working with the 2004 Symposium.

Regarding the article request, Kristen Renn from Michigan State agreed to write the article about out SSAOs for the *Leadership Exchange* (Volume One, Issue Four, Fall 2003). The article was published, but it was disappointing that there was not one out person on the 2004 Manicur Symposium faculty. The issues of being lesbian and an SSAO were only briefly addressed at the opening of the symposium and a few copies of the Renn *Leadership Exchange* article were made available at the back of the room. Nothing further was mentioned throughout the week. As a lesbian, I felt a deep sense of unimportance, especially since I knew that names had been forwarded. Once again I felt invisible, left out, devalued, and less than the other women present.

There was one moment at that symposium, however, that is engraved in my mind forever. One morning we were told that we could identify topics for lunch table discussions. Someone wishing to discuss a particular topic could announce that topic, and others who wanted to participate could attend that table. I felt so proud when one young professional stood up and announced a table called "Out of the closet and into the SSAO boardroom." That was such a courageous move for this young professional, who is not very open about her sexual identity. Surprisingly, the table was full, and I honestly believe that there were others who wanted to sit with us but were afraid. That lunch was one of the most valuable times for me during that entire symposium. NASPA missed a valuable opportunity at that symposium to make a difference and a statement, especially among senior student affairs officers who must be the role models for their staff and for our students. I will raise this topic again at the board to create more movement in this direction.

While it is critical that professional associations address the issue of LGBT SSAOs who are reluctant to be visible in the profession, it is just as important that they assure our midlevel managers and young professionals that they can be out, be honest about who they are in their entirety, and not have to take a nose-dive back into the closet should they desire promotion into senior positions.

Recently, via e-mail, Sanlo asked members of the National Consortium of Directors of LGBT Resources in Higher Education this question: As LGBT professionals in student affairs, what do you expect of your student affairs professional organizations? Their responses follow in no prioritized order:

- Written, visible nondiscriminatory membership policies to include sexual orientation and gender identity or expression
- LGBT-specific conference programming
- LGBT issues reflected in publications and research (published articles must be inclusive regardless of the topic)
- Funding for LGBT student affairs research
- Immediate organizational response to national LGBT issues that affect higher education
- Support for the expansion of graduate-level curriculum for full inclusion of the issues and lives of LGBT students and staff
- Capacity-building workshops with LGBT centers
- LGBT career seminars about advancement in higher education
- Graduate internships in LGBT centers
- Recognition of LGBT-related research conducted by graduate students
- Mentoring programs for LGBT undergraduates as they consider student affairs as a career choice
- Out SSAOs as role models and mentors
- Opportunities to introduce graduate students to LGBT higher education work
- Greater effort by non-LGBT SSAOs to mentor LGBT professionals
- Removal of the lavender ceiling
- Discontinuation of the discriminatory practice, conscious or otherwise, of hosting regional and annual conferences in cities that do not have sexual orientation in their nondiscrimination policy

Embracing the LGBT Summit, now Institute, is a great beginning, but we cannot rest on that. We must make sure that the annual conference career placement centers are welcoming places for our LGBT members, prohibiting employers that do not have nondiscrimination policies regarding sexual orientation. Professional associations also have a responsibility to provide professional development opportunities for people who will be supervising entry-level and midlevel professionals; they also need to be more directed in professional development offerings. SSAO workshops or summer multiday training specifically on LGBT issues would be a giant step forward. The challenges, of course, are pinpointing where the need is, identifying a captive audience, and determining who will provide the training. Typically, the people who need LGBT training do not attend.

A bonus of being involved with professional associations on the national level is getting to know the organization and the leaders. As rank-and-file members, we often just watch our leaders at conferences and from a distance. At best we read someone's biography online as they run for national office. It's rare that we actually get to spend time with them individually, and even more rare to know what they really believe, what guides them in this work.

I have been fortunate as a professional and as a lesbian to get to know some of our leaders. But there are so many of my LGBT colleagues who do not know their leaders, and certainly do not know that they are valued by our organization. They need to know. Student affairs professional associations must step out more loudly and more courageously, take risks regarding LGBT issues, and be the social change leaders that they can and must be. I know that the core values are there. I know that the people who care are there. It's time for NASPA, ACPA (American College Personnel Association), and all of the student affairs associations to act.

Gwen's Story

Confronting the challenges of culture and politics in professional organizations is both daunting and critical. One such challenge is to create a climate where professionals who identify as lesbian, gay, bisexual, or transgender (LGBT) know that they have the needed support if they choose to be open about their sexual orientation or gender identity and that they are being treated fairly by being afforded the same benefits of membership as all other members. This challenge is one that professional organizations will enthusiastically tackle if they want to thrive as leaders within the higher education community.

One might ask what makes creating this supportive climate a challenge? The challenge is that an organization is inseparable from its members. Though the entity welcomes all members regardless of their sexual orientation or gender identity, some individual members may choose not to attempt to transcend their personal biases towards LGBT members. Therefore, it is incumbent on the organizations' leadership to find ways to continue the conversations around our multiple diversities and invisible identities. In doing so, members will acknowledge that organizations are not neutral; that their corporate actions communicate what is important; and, consequently, that issues of access for traditionally marginalized groups must be addressed or organizations run the risk of reproducing the status quo.

The Importance of LGBT Professionals in Leadership Roles. An organization is not serving all of its members well if LGBT members are not represented on committees and task forces, are not nominated to run for office, or are seldom asked to speak at conferences and meetings. Further, an organization could be seen as failing in its responsibility when professionals assume that the reason that they are not promoted or selected for a high-level administrative position is that they openly identify as lesbian, gay, bisexual, or transgender.

The reality is that not only is the organization reneging on its promise of benefits to membership, it is missing an opportunity to tap into a rich pool of talent for leadership and for role modeling for students and newer professionals entering the field. It is also missing the opportunity to develop heterosexual allies as role models as well.

Professional Organizations as Advocates. Professional organizations should provide the mechanism by which members "become known" and have the opportunity to network for personal and institutional support. It is not unusual to hear senior student affairs officers (SSAO) describe the important role of the contacts made through their professional organization as fundamental to their positioning in the field and to their ongoing need for information and consultation. The role of professional organizations extends in many directions; it includes the formulation of research agendas and emerging policy needs as well as the advocacy issues pursued on behalf of the membership.

Though it is risky for some organizations because of the beliefs of some of its members, a primary role of a professional organization is advocacy on behalf of all of its members. As I write about student affairs professional organizations and their responsibilities to LGBT student affairs professionals, I am aware that my perspective is influenced by my own experiences as a member of professional organizations. As an African American woman from a working poor family, I have lived within the dynamic tensions created by the intersections of race, class, and gender. The circumscriptions of these sociological identifiers have contributed to what I might have perceived as negative attitudinal and behavioral reactions toward me from my fellow members. What I experienced were more than likely cultural practices embedded in the norms of a particular time in the organizational evolution that had not yet adapted as the demographics of the membership were changing. This is why it is so important that, as groups that have historically been marginalized become members of professional organizations, efforts are made to ensure that these groups do not remain marginalized in the organization. In order to include LGBT professionals more fully, leaders and members of organizations must examine the embedded value of heterosexism in everyday structures that tend to exclude individuals who do not fit the norm. For example, simple corrections to language on membership forms and on invitations to events are part of adapting to the changes necessary to accommodate all members.

The dominant paradigm sets the tone for what issues get addressed, who is chosen to provide leadership for everything from board membership to selection of conference themes and planners, and what kinds of professional development occur. Inclusion in national projects, in research projects, as conference speakers, and as editorial board members all are aspects of the organization that communicate value.

Since organizational structure and culture are shaped by the membership, it's imperative that those who hold leadership roles develop strategies to work with the membership to articulate and demonstrate through actions values of equity and inclusiveness for all members. In other words, relationships to power and privilege in the organization must never be based on sociological identifiers such as race, class, gender, and sexual orientation. Transparency in how opportunities are afforded members is one way to demonstrate equity among the membership.

Exclusivity versus Inclusion. Essentially, professionals come together under the umbrella of an organization to consider how they want their profession to evolve. They want to participate in shaping and reshaping the field in which they are working. I learned to value the fact that professionals would organize themselves to work on increasing the quality of their own development, to generate knowledge for the profession, to share resources, and to form communities of gifted experts working together toward shared goals for the greater good.

It is through participating in such activities that members solidify their professional identity. However, the risk and reward inherent in a gathering of people with something in common is that the group will become exclusive. Exclusivity is positive in bringing people together for the purpose of attending to the quality and growth of a professional field of study and practice. However, if exclusivity within the organization begins to mirror or reflect the social and political context of the broader society where difference is marginalized, it is the responsibility of leaders and all members of the organization, especially one built on a foundation of teaching and acquisition of knowledge, to demand an examination of internalized prejudices that are often subconscious and sometimes become overt in actions and decisions.

A viable professional organization must continuously adapt to the demographic changes among its membership. It must not only state that it values diversity, it must continue to self-examine, admit mistakes, and take bold actions to ensure that the organization is structured both to benefit its diverse membership and to benefit from the diverse perspectives of its members.

As I was finding my place in professional organizations early in my career, during a time when the doors were opening wider for racial and ethnic diversity, I would often find myself representing my race whether I chose to or not. It was also obvious that I was present but not visible to those who held the power to share all the privileges of membership. If those of us who were different called attention to what we perceived as inequitable treatment, the question would sometimes be, What do those people want? What we wanted was the promise of membership.

The Responsibilities of Professional Organizations to the LGBT Community. Wall and Evans (2000) contend there are three themes that capture institution-wide concerns of LGBT individuals: visibility, normalcy, and equity. These themes provide an excellent summary for considering the responsibilities of a professional organization to the LGBT community. Continuous review of organizational policies and practices related to the visibility of LGBT issues is important. Research agendas, conference sessions, policy discussions, leadership, and advocacy are all avenues to increase LGBT visibility. The normalcy of LGBT individuals is reinforced when LGBT people are part of the everyday fabric of an organization. Research continues to demonstrate that knowing someone gay is a key to being supportive of the rights of LGBT individuals and to becoming allies (Wall and Evans, 2000). Professional organizations can advocate strongly for efforts to create safe spaces for open LGBT staff and students. As well, the organization itself must pay attention to the kind of safe space it creates for increasing the visibility and leadership opportunities for openly LGBT professionals. And finally, issues of equity must be at the center of a professional organization's agenda. The professional organization must advocate for the fair treatment of all individuals.

Professional organizations are situated in the midst of many societal tensions, and they mirror the struggle for promoting social justice and ensuring personal equity. As with other traditionally marginalized groups, LGBT students, staff, and faculty have much to offer our learning communities. The profession will ultimately benefit from the strong and consistent support of the professional organization related to issues of justice. Our ability as professional organizations to create, use, and model vibrant, inclusive practices and to struggle with the hard issues of the day will model the leadership necessary for campuses to provide services for students that treat members fairly and provide opportunities for LGBT staff, administrators, and students to find their voice.

References

Wall, V., and Evans, N. (eds.). *Toward Acceptance: Sexual Orientation Issues on Campus.* Washington, D.C.: American College Personnel Association, 2000.

JUDITH A. ALBIN *is senior associate director of unions and student activities at Pennsylvania State University and national chair of the NASPA Knowledge Communities.*

GWENDOLYN JORDAN DUNGY *is executive director of the National Association of Student Personnel Administrators (NASPA).*

INDEX

Back Issue/Subscription Order Form

Copy or detach and send to:
Jossey-Bass, A Wiley Imprint, 989 Market Street, San Francisco CA, 94103-1741

Call or fax toll-free: Phone 888-378-2537 6:30AM – 3PM PST; Fax 888-481-2665

Back Issues: Please send me the following issues at $27 each
(Important: Please include ISBN number with your order.)

_____

_____

_____

$ _____   Total for single issues

$ _____   SHIPPING CHARGES: SURFACE   Domestic Canadian
                                    First Item $5.00 $6.00
                                    Each Add'l Item $3.00 $1.50
                 For next-day and second-day delivery rates, call the number listed above.

Subscriptions   Please __ start __ renew my subscription to *New Directions for Student Services* for the year 2_____at the following rate:

U.S.	__ Individual $75	__ Institutional $170
Canada	__ Individual $75	__ Institutional $210
All Others	__ Individual $99	__ Institutional $244

**For more information about online subscriptions visit
www.wileyinterscience.com**

$
_____   Total single issues and subscriptions (Add appropriate sales tax for your state for single issue orders. No sales tax for U.S. subscriptions. Canadian residents, add GST for subscriptions and single issues.)

__Payment enclosed (U.S. check or money order only)

__VISA __ MC __ AmEx Card #_____Exp. Date_____

Signature _____ Day Phone _____

__Bill Me (U.S. institutional orders only. Purchase order required.)

Purchase order # _____
                 Federal Tax ID13559302   **GST 89102 8052**

Name _____

Address _____

_____

Phone _____ E-mail _____

For more information about Jossey-Bass, visit our Web site at www.josseybass.com

SS110   **Developing Social Justice Allies**
Robert D. Reason, Ellen M. Broido, Tracy L. Davis, Nancy J. Evans
Social justice allies are individuals from dominant groups (for example,
whites, heterosexuals, men) who work to end the oppression of target group
members (people of color, homosexuals, women). Student affairs
professionals have a history of philosophical commitment to social justice,
and this volume strives to provide the theoretical foundation and practical
strategies to encourage the development of social justice and civil rights
allies among students and colleagues.
ISBN: 0-7879-8077-3

SS109   **Serving Native American Students**
Mary Jo Tippeconnic Fox, Shelly C. Lowe, George S. McClellan
The increasing Native American enrollment on campuses nationwide is
something to celebrate; however, the retention rate for Native American
students is the lowest in higher education, a point of tremendous concern.
This volume's authors—most of them Native American—address topics such
as enrollment trends, campus experiences, cultural traditions, student
services, ignorance about Indian country issues, expectations of tribal
leaders and parents, and other challenges and opportunities encountered by ·
Native students.
ISBN: 0-7879-7971-6

SS108   **Using Entertainment Media in Student Affairs Teaching and Practice**
Deanna S. Forney, Tony W. Cawthon
Reaching all students may require going beyond traditional methods,
especially in the out-of-classroom environments typical to student affairs.
Using films, music, television shows, and popular books can help students
learn. This volume—good for both practitioners and educators—shares
effective approaches to using entertainment media to facilitate
understanding of general student development, multiculturalism, sexual
orientation, gender issues, leadership, counseling, and more.
ISBN: 0-7879-7926-0

SS107   **Developing Effective Programs and Services for College Men**
Gar E. Kellom
This volume's aim is to better understand the challenges facing college men,
particularly at-risk men. Topics include enrollment, retention, academic
performance, women's college perspectives, men's studies perspectives,
men's health issues, emotional development, and spirituality. Delivers
recommendations and examples about programs and services that improve
college men's learning experiences and race, class, and gender awareness.
ISBN: 0-7879-7772-1

SS106   **Serving the Millennial Generation**
Michael D. Coomes, Robert DeBard
Focuses on the next enrollment boom, students born after 1981, known as
the Millennial generation. Examines these students' attitudes, beliefs, and

behaviors, and makes recommendations to student affairs practitioners for working with them. Discusses historical and cultural influences that shape generations, demographics, teaching and learning patterns of Millennials, and how student affairs can best educate and serve them.
ISBN: 0-7879-7606-7

SS105   **Addressing the Unique Needs of Latino American Students**
Anna M. Ortiz
Explores the experiences of the fast-growing population of Latinos in higher education, and what these students need from student affairs. This volume examines the influence of the Latino family, socioeconomic levels, cultural barriers, and other factors to understand the challenges faced by Latinos. Discusses administration, student groups, community colleges, support programs, cultural identity, Hispanic-Serving Institutions, and more.
ISBN: 0-7879-7479-X

SS104   **Meeting the Needs of African American Women**
Mary F. Howard-Hamilton
Identifies and explores the critical needs for African American women as students, faculty, and administrators. This volume introduces theoretical frameworks and practical applications for addressing challenges; discusses identity and spirituality; explores the importance of programming support in recruitment and retention; describes the benefits of mentoring; and provides illuminating case studies of black women's issues in higher education.
ISBN: 0-7879-7280-0

SS103   **Contemporary Financial Issues in Student Affairs**
John H. Schuh
This volume addresses the challenging financial situation facing higher education and offers creative solutions for student affairs staff. Topics include the differences between public and private institutions in funding student activities, how to demonstrate financial accountability to stakeholders, plus ways to address budget challenges in student unions, health centers, campus recreation, counseling centers, and student housing.
ISBN: 0-7879-7173-1

SS102   **Meeting the Special Needs of Adult Students**
Deborah Kilgore, Penny J. Rice
This volume examines the ways student services professionals can best help adult learners. Chapters highlight the specific challenges that adult enrollment brings to traditional four-year and postgraduate institutions, which are often focused on the traditional-aged student experience. Explaining that adult students are typically involved in campus life in different ways than younger students are, the volume provides student services professionals with good guidance on serving an ever-growing population.
ISBN: 0-7879-6991-5

NEW DIRECTIONS FOR STUDENT SERVICES
IS NOW AVAILABLE ONLINE AT WILEY INTERSCIENCE

What is Wiley InterScience?

Wiley InterScience is the dynamic online content service from John Wiley & Sons delivering the full text of over 300 leading scientific, technical, medical, and professional journals, plus major reference works, the acclaimed *Current Protocols* laboratory manuals, and even the full text of select Wiley print books online.

What are some special features of Wiley InterScience?

Wiley InterScience Alerts is a service that delivers table of contents via e-mail for any journal available on Wiley InterScience as soon as a new issue is published online.
Early View is Wiley's exclusive service presenting individual articles online as soon as they are ready, even before the release of the compiled print issue. These articles are complete, peer-reviewed, and citable.
CrossRef is the innovative multi-publisher reference linking system enabling readers to move seamlessly from a reference in a journal article to the cited publication, typically located on a different server and published by a different publisher.

How can I access Wiley InterScience?

Visit http://www.interscience.wiley.com

Guest Users can browse Wiley InterScience for unrestricted access to journal Tables of Contents and Article Abstracts, or use the powerful search engine.
Registered Users are provided with a *Personal Home Page* to store and manage customized alerts, searches, and links to favorite journals and articles. Additionally, Registered Users can view free Online Sample Issues and preview selected material from major reference works.
Licensed Customers are entitled to access full-text journal articles in PDF, with select journals also offering full-text HTML.

How do I become an Authorized User?

Authorized Users are individuals authorized by a paying Customer to have access to the journals in Wiley InterScience. For example, a university that subscribes to Wiley journals is considered to be the Customer. Faculty, staff and students authorized by the university to have access to those journals in Wiley InterScience are Authorized Users. Users should contact their Library for information on which Wiley journals they have access to in Wiley InterScience.

ASK YOUR INSTITUTION ABOUT WILEY INTERSCIENCE TODAY!

CPSIA information can be obtained at www.ICGtesting.com
Printed in the USA
BVOW04s1341270114

343066BV00001B/1/A